HOW TO GET BEAUTIFUL WOMEN...
And Everything Else You Want From Life

By: Matthew C. Horne

Optimum Success International
Post Office Box 441328
Fort Washington, MD 20744-4109

Orders@matthewchorne.com
http://www.matthewchorne.com

All rights reserved. No part of this book may be reproduced or transmitted in any form or by any means—electronic, mechanical, photocopying, recording, or otherwise—without written permission from the author, except for the inclusion of brief quotations in a review.

The author of this book provides information for attaining success and living your best life possible. The provided information is based on the personal philosophy of the author. The intent is to offer general information that, when applied, will aid the reader in his quest for maximizing his human potential and self-discovery. In the event that you use any of the information in this book, the author and publisher assume no responsibility for your actions.

Copyright © 2013

Matthew C. Horne, Optimum Success International Publishing
All rights reserved.

Printed in the United States of America
ISBN 978-0-9794550-3-2 0-9794550-3-0

DEDICATION

I would like to dedicate this book to my late aunt, Brenda Horne. Thank you for making every gathering that much more enjoyable and fun. Thank you for making me feel like the most handsome man in the world, from as far back as I can remember. If I learned anything from you, it's to be unafraid to create new beginnings, and to flat out live my life, while having fun doing so.

I would also like to thank my parents, Bernard and Valerie Horne for their unending support of, and belief in, me.

I would also like to thank my followers and supporters for giving me an ever- increasing voice in the self-development industry.

A special dedication goes out to all of the young black motivational speakers who paved the way for me to believe I could begin my journey in this industry before I graduated from college. You all kept a positive outlook in me at the onset of my journey, when my college professors didn't believe I would graduate. I would like to thank motivational legend, Les Brown, for endorsing my books, The Universe Is Inviting You In and All We Have is NOW. Every time I hear you speak, you reinvigorate my personal power. Thank you, Ona Brown, for being very instrumental in getting me endorsed by your father so early in my career, and for just being the light bearing person you are.

I would also like to thank my family for supporting my work and spreading the word to all who will listen. Thank you mom, for being my one-woman marketing team! I am thankful to both of my late grandmothers Ida Hardy and Dillie Horne for serving as the matriarchs of my family.

Lastly, I would like to thank the all-knowing omniscient Creator for giving me a gift to touch the lives of the masses, and walk them to the doorstep of their limitless possibilities.

TABLE OF CONTENTS

Preface 7

Chapter 1: Why Fear a Pretty Face? 9

Chapter 2: The Allure of the Game 19

Chapter 3: Appearance 33

Chapter 4: Late Model Luxury 43

Chapter 5: The Success Undershirt 55

Chapter 6: Energy 65

Chapter 7: The Dating Game 83

Chapter 8: Play To Win 95

Chapter 9: Play Your Hand 109

Chapter 10: Egypt or Genesis 123

PREFACE

With many men feeling as if incredibly beautiful women and the various aspirations they have for their life are: "out of their league," I felt the need to bridge the gap between men and the highest desires they experience.

My belief is that nothing is beyond our grasp in life, as long as we have the audacity to approach it. This is not a "how to be a player" guide. If that's your thing, then go for it playboy. The permeating belief is as you become a better man with a larger vision, you will naturally attract the various things you want from life - including beautiful women.

When my friends would observe the beautiful women I frequently interacted with, I would always let them know that having aesthetic wonders is not something that is exclusive to just me - relaying a belief that they possess the same ability to attract the unparalleled beauties they desire. I've done my share of dating beautiful women, and quite frankly, my findings are unveiled with every turn of the page.

In totality, this book is not about getting beautiful women; it's about having an awareness of yourself that awakens you to your ability to create virtually anything you want for your life.

Self-actualization is at the root of this book. If you have a strong belief in, and awareness of, how unlimited you really are, you will encounter everything you want from life - with beautiful women just being a complement to the overall life you desire to live.

With one shot at this thing called life, it makes sense to entertain the highest desires you have. This book is about becoming fearless, and never stopping until you find your matches in life that bring you optimal levels of peace and fulfillment.

Life is your blank canvas; Allow *How to Get Beautiful Women and Everything Else You Want From Life* guide you on how to paint your vision on it.

CHAPTER 1:
WHY FEAR A PRETTY FACE?

As one of my good friends and I engaged in conversation, he told me about a jaw-dropping traffic-stopper of a women, who walked through a supermarket where he was shopping. In his description of this event on that day, every man who caught a glimpse of this woman acted as if time had stopped. Cashiers stopped what they were doing; men with their wife and kids paused in admiration; other men re-routed their shopping paths to catch an additional glimpse of this woman, in hopes of just keeping a mental snap-shot.

He then went on to tell me that no one said a word to her. By intelligent deductive reasoning, she was more than desired by the men she encountered, and it's safe to say that not every man belonged to another woman. I began to think: what could have kept these men from approaching her? It was simply a fear of her beauty.

Being a young man in my late twenties, I still enjoy a night on the town from time to time. My observant nature keeps my eyes open to the realities that surround me, no matter where I am. Night life in Washington D.C. can be intimidating for any man, given the influx of beautiful women who infiltrate the clubs. It's a consensus from out-of-town visitors: D.C. has some of the most beautiful and accomplished women in the U.S. You will be out and see some of the most beautiful women you've ever seen in person, on any given night of the week.

What perplexes me is some men's unwillingness to approach these women. You can tell in a man's demeanor, when a woman he desires crosses his path. At that moment it's like I'm watching the movie The Hunger Games, and I'm observing subjects from afar to see their reaction to a situation. I'm cheering the man on: "Come on, say something to her." Much to my dismay, most men just let these types of women pass them by, caused by inner-doubt. In reality, it could also be to the dismay of the woman who saw your interest, which she happened to share.

A hesitant step will always land you in the sea of normalcy, flooded with men who choose not to act when an inner push moves them towards the woman they desire.

Approach her ...She's Waiting

If beautiful women did not want to be approached by you, especially in a late night social environment, they wouldn't spend hours in the mirror glamorizing their appearance. Is she doing this for you, or her girlfriends she'll be hanging with that night, who are more than familiar with her? The answer is: you! I can't count how many women I've seen still adjusting their makeup as they attempt to find parking near a night spot. Believe me; she has your approach in mind when she's doing this.

Even if the woman is taken, she still enjoys the satisfaction of a man's approach; it lets her know she's still in demand. Every visual enhancement a woman performs on herself is subconsciously to attract men. We are hard wired to do things to attract the opposite sex, even if it's not on a conscious level.

There's Power in the Word "No"

A man's primary obstacle in the pursuit of beautiful women is "rejection." I've played some professional basketball and have hung out with NBA players in night clubs. Believe it or not, women tell them "No." At a much lesser rate than the average Joe, but it happens to every man - if he's ever placed himself in the game of pursuing what he wants in terms of women. Later in the book, I will show you how to be irresistible to any type of woman, creating a highly probable "yes" when you approach them.

Hearing the word "no" from a woman, after expressing your desire to further the conversation, does two things for you: It educates you on how to create a "yes," and positions you to find a match. If you hear enough "no's," it's an indirect education on how to consistently create the "yes" you desire. The word "no," if heard enough, will reveal to you why you keep hearing it. As you keep reading, you will learn how to create a "yes" before you even open your mouth.

An ego will dissuade a man from approaching a woman because of the mere possibility she will say "no." This is a sad existence, for if you are led by your ego, you will never approach the woman you want. You will have to navigate your way through some rejection in order to find your match. If you are led by your ego, it's almost impossible to navigate your way to a "yes."

Allow me to imbed this theory. I was at a night spot not too long ago, and I attempted to talk to a girl who pretty much ignored me. She was nice looking, but not categorically gorgeous. In walks this woman who was flawless. I took the approach that my previous encounter was just a miss-match. So I literally and figuratively pivoted from the miss- matched encounter, took a couple of steps, and began talking to the flawless beauty. Our energy was undeniable, resulting in us going out the next day.

What if I had put my tail between my legs because the first woman rejected me? Or worse yet, what if my ego would have said: "Don't approach any more women tonight, because it's lame to put yourself in a vulnerable position and experience rejection again?" I furthered the conversation with the most beautiful woman in the club because I had a short memory of my previous encounter, and pivoted into the best situation possible.

In the game of basketball, a scoring champion is crowned every year. They score more points than every other player, but underneath it all, they take more shots.

If you desire beautiful women, the only way to win your championship is to continuously shoot the ball; continuously pull the trigger when an opportunity arises for you take the perfect shot.

Recently, I was doing a book signing for two of my previous books at a prominent outdoor venue. I had a young guy with me that day, who is like a brother to me. He observed a stunningly-beautiful woman with a man one would ideally not perceive to be a match for her beauty. She essentially appeared to be out of his league. My young brother asked me, with a look of perplexity, "How did he get her?" I immediately replied: "Because he approached her." He had to get the conversation started at some point, which began with an initial approach. What my little brother and I experienced was the end result of that approach: them taking a leisurely weekend stroll arm in arm.

My stance remains the same: Why fear a pretty face? In my elementary years, my dad told me, "The worst thing a girl will ever tell you is "no."" The antithesis to this statement is, the best thing a girl will ever tell you is "yes."

.....And everything else you want from life

Most people do not get the things they want from life because they are afraid to approach them. It's not always the best, the brightest, or the most qualified that makes it to the top. Often times it's the person who believes they belong there. To get the things you want from life, you must begin with a belief that you deserve them.

To be a solid man, you must be sold on yourself before anyone, or anything, else outside of God. Maslow's Hierarchy of Human Needs suggests that of all the needs of human beings, self actualization is the most important. Essentially he is saying a strong sense of self is the highest asset you can possess as a human being.

Life is full of ebbs and flows, ups and downs, hot and cold periods, as this is the cycle of life. If you have a strong sense of self, it is difficult to be knocked off your core beliefs, which are the foundation to build the life you desire.

If you have a strong sense of self, the word "no" is never a deterrent in the pursuit of what you want; it simply means you have yet to find a match. After all, you are deserving of what you want. There's only one you, and will only be one you, so what sense does it make to sell yourself short and allow the fear of opposition rob you of the possibilities of living in your life's vision? The highest functioning human beings have a strong sense of self. This is not based in narcissism, but rather in not settling for less than they deserve in life.

The Power of Vision

A solid man will always have a vision, something higher than he has yet to achieve, which guides him. A very popular book states, "Where there is no vision, the people perish." The antithesis to this statement is, "Where there is vision, the people flourish."

We are hardwired to stay the course towards the vision that consumes us. Whatever fixates in your thoughts is what you will put energy into, and by default, create. Develop a vision of where you would like your life to go, as this is the beginning of living the life you want to live. It's an aimless existence to live a life without vision. It's a limitless existence to live a life with a vision.

You cannot stop until you get what you want from life. I would be selling you a false dream to say that you can become anything you want to be in life. If you are non-athletic and over-the-hill, there's no future in professional sports. But I guarantee you that you possess God-given attributes that can take you places, if you develop a vision.

En route to your destination, you will encounter your share of "no's." Everyone will not share your sense of self and vision, which is perfectly fine.

No one is born with the lens of clarity that you were given to see your dreams, abilities and desires.

If people can't see you in your most divine state of purpose, why give them power to cloud your lens of clarity? A sense of self is not allowing anyone, or anything, to dissuade you from living your life's passion.

Abraham Maslow could conclude that self actualization is the most vital of all human needs, because something will always be in place to shrink your perception of yourself. Do whatever it takes to create and maintain a strong sense of your potential, and never compromise it, which creates the chance of making it your reality.

That Magical Door

You never know which door leads to the opportunities that you desire from life. It's a matter of continuously and fearlessly approaching them until you find a match. If one door closes, or doesn't quite open, maintain the perspective that all you need is one match for magic to begin to happen in your life.

When you put your energy into something, there is a magic called providence that begins to draw you closer to whatever you intend to create for your life. You will find yourself in the right place, at the right time, meeting the right people, to make your vision a reality - when you choose to stay the course, with no thought of your surroundings. Providence is the provisions that are on your path to guide you to your intended destination.

Your match is out there. Keep moving forward until you find it. If you are tempted to be discouraged by anything you leave behind when you pursue your vision, remember that if you didn't desire something new, you would have never left the past, in the past.

You don't deserve the things that you want from life because you are the best or the brightest; you deserve them because you are you. You are a person with the power to create a vision and ultimately live in it.

I encourage you take the shots that you desire to take in life. A shooter will always shoot the ball, no matter if they are hot or cold. A high achiever will always seek new opportunities to succeed, despite the end result of their last venture. Every moment given to you is an opportunity to create a genesis. Detach yourself from your past, and immerse yourself in the possibilities each moment of life gives to create what you want from life.

My college coach always highlighted the All-American on my team. He said this player had a short memory, whether he made or missed a shot. His approach remained the same: he unwaveringly attacked the game, which created the outcome of him being named one of the top fifty players in all of college basketball. Sure, he made mistakes, didn't always get the outcomes he desired through the course of the game, but underneath it all, his mindset did not change.

There is more to you than you could ever imagine. Life is not worth living if you aren't pushing the boundaries of what's possible for you. Do you see yourself as deserving of the desires that burn deep within you? Or does fear blanket them, keeping you frozen? When you make it to the end, one thing you will realize is that your breakthrough wasn't as far out there as you first perceived it to be. Approach her ....she's waiting.

NOTES AND INSIGHTS

CHAPTER 2:
THE ALLURE OF THE GAME

What do beautiful women respond to? It's the allure that surrounds a man. A man with a vision is far more attractive than a man who is just meandering through life.

Allure is the byproduct of the intrigue that is created when a woman encounters a man who lives outside of the norms of society.

Don't accept the status quo and the norm as your plight in life. Always reach towards something greater than you have yet to accomplish. If you work a job, work on starting your own business. Living outside of the box has more appeal to women than you could ever imagine. A man with a vision is the object of affection for any woman.

Be Who You Say You Are

In Washington, D.C., and many other major cities, everyone is a star if you hear them tell it. Stunting is very prevalent, with inflated occupational tales being tossed in women's faces, with the hope of impressing them. Eventually these types of men get found out quickly, due to superfast cell phones with internet that lead to a little website called Google.com. Believe it; women will "Google" you instantly if you say you are someone who has an out-of-the-box occupation. In my experience, some will wait a few moments, while others will Google you right in your face, to see if you are who you say you are.

One woman I dated simply said, that with all of the talking bobble heads she had encountered, she had never met anyone who was actually who they said they were. She was more than impressed, with her energy suggesting that she wanted to know even more about me. Allure will tip the scale in your favor, because it speaks volumes about you without saying a word. A beautiful woman will discard the droves of men who worship her, with a pursuit that lands them in the sea of normalcy. She's looking for a man who is different - with his accomplishments having a momentum that lets her know she can't play the same games with you, that she plays with the normal men she encounters. Beautiful women, as a result of their daily adoration from men, are rarely intrigued by them. I will show you how to be the man she desires.

Success is something that should not be worn on your sleeve. There is nothing more unattractive to a woman than a man who boasts about his occupation or bank account, when she didn't solicit this type of information during a conversation. If you are who you say you are, your allure will speak for you in the initial moments when you two encounter one another.

> *Insecure men lead in with what they do for a living and what they have. A quietly confident man is sold on himself, not acquisitions or material wealth.*

She'll be more than intrigued if she can peel you back in layers, with each revelation of you being more enticing than the next. If you have to lead in with what you do, who you are, or what you have, your identity is outside of you. Ultimately, material possessions can leave just as fast as they came. If you are sold on you, and a woman is sold on you before the material world enters the conversation, chances are you are poised for something lasting. Who you are will eventually come up in conversation, but let it come up. Just relax and let Google.com talk for you. The only way this can happen is to go out there and create something more for yourself.

It is a precious gift to be able to create the life you envision living, so what better moment than NOW to chart a path to your desired destination?

The dichotomy of getting beautiful women is that being wrapped up in your life's purpose and vision is so attractive to women, that they naturally want you without all of the chasing and courting. Momentum is the scent that infatuates beautiful women. If you are progressing towards your life's vision, they understand from the moment they lay eyes on you, that they will likely be left behind if they attempt to engage you in a chase.

Allure makes a beautiful woman look at you eye to eye, instead of looking down at the normal man who views her in adoration, on her pedestal.

Being lost in women leads to a perpetual chase. Being lost in yourself, and what you can accomplish for your life, creates a flow in your interaction with beautiful women. These aren't games, but concrete truths I've encountered through my years of dating, and by observing other men.

Be a Solid Man

Beautiful women will test you to see whether or not you are a solid man. Large numbers of men turn feminine when a beautiful woman tests them to see if his sense of self is more important than her flawless looks. Many men tolerate ill-advised behavior from beautiful women because they subconsciously believe she is out of their league, and they are undeserving of her.

I recently was dating a true-to-life five-foot ten inch beautiful model. She was cool, but was into herself a little too much. In typical beautiful women, big city fashion, she let me know of a certain professional athlete who harasses her via the phone. She claimed she wasn't into the guy. I was like: "Oh that's cool." The comedic element was that a large number of the beautiful women I've dated have gone out of their way to tell me how this guy pursued them. In their mind they think they're special because someone of that caliber would pursue them, while in reality he's just taking shots with reckless abandon. She, as well as the other women I dated, all said they rejected his advances. This is their way of saying: "Look at me! I not only get pursued by pro athletes, I also turn them down." So this is the first date with the model.

We hit it off quickly, and found ourselves alone on a Friday night enjoying each other's company. Right on cue, she tells me that this particular athlete called her. I told her that she should go on a date with the guy. A look of perplexity graced her face. I said, "I know the guy, and he's a good dude. You've mentioned him frequently in the short time we've known one another, so why not give it a shot? He's obviously on your mind." All of this was said with no emotion or change of expression. Emotion, in a situation like this, is a sign of weakness. It means she got under your skin.

This was not the response she was expecting. And once again, I wasn't playing any games. I think games are for losers. It was just my honest thought. She responded with, "But I'm here with you."

If you are solid, when she tests you, a passing grade will always be given. Many guys in that situation would have been offended, and let it show. If you are centered in yourself, you will say exactly what I said. When you've given her your energy and undivided attention, by not throwing things in her face, the same respect should be reciprocated. You simply can't be afraid to lose her.

The man, who is unafraid to lose her, will always have her.

Men literally walk on egg shells around these women, but self-assurance reveals a comfort with her and yourself that she is not used to experiencing.

Self-assurance translates into intrigue. Intrigue is the gateway to allure. If your allure is strong enough, she'll be caught up in your rapture.

Who in the world would tell a legitimate runway model to go ahead and date someone else, after she continues to mention the guy? You! Because you know in your core that her pretty face does not override your sense of self. Your sense of self will continually be mentioned throughout this book, because it is the core of creating balanced interaction with beautiful women, as well as creating a balanced life.

Chapter 2: THE ALLURE OF THE GAME

Leverage

A beautiful woman will always be intrigued by you if she knows her looks don't give her leverage over you.

Allure exists when no matter how drop dead gorgeous she is, the playing field is still level between the two of you. In her core she wants a man who will meet her eye-to-eye, and not admire her on her pedestal. She actually wants the man who will kick her pedestal and allow her to land safely in his arms.

She wants the man who doesn't always say "yes" to her, but possesses a mind of his own.

Many people believe you have to be rude and obnoxious to get a beautiful woman to respect you. In reality, all you have to do is politely let her know when she's stepped out of bounds, and just be cool. Just talk to her in the straight lines most men are afraid to, and your allure will overwhelm her.

.....And everything else you want from life

Allure is the momentum of a man who is not afraid to step outside of society's box and create something for himself. The man who is not afraid to be himself, and constantly pushes the boundaries of life, is desirable not just to women, but people as a whole. Confidence and audacity are traits that people sorely lack in our society. In most cases, from the time you are a kid, mental conditioning teaches you to grow up and play it safe in life. When people encounter the rare individual who lives life on their own terms, they will naturally gravitate towards you, wanting a piece of you.

Allure is a fixture in the life of any high-achiever, because they never stop creating new ways to challenge themselves, unveiling new facets from within they never knew existed. We were created to push the boundaries of life.

Guard Your Space

When your life ambitions go from being dreams to actual realities, the world around you will change. It is my desire that you will find yourself in the category of an alluring man, because if this is the case for you, you are climbing life's escalator.

Just as allure is a force that is celebrated by many, there will be an equal amount of people who despise your life's progress - as you reap the benefits of the risks they were afraid to take in life.

In a conscious human mind everyone, to a degree, feels special because of the individuality of there being only one you. Many people think that their accomplishments are greater than what they actually are. I submit to you, that you haven't left society's box until someone you least expect turns on you. When your life truly reaches a place where you've created a separation so drastic from the people who were once on the same level as you, someone will turn on you.

Success, on the level that it creates allure, will offend some people. If your success hasn't offended anyone, then even if you began making a separation from people who were familiar with you "back when," you are barely off the ground.

Further in this book, I will discuss how you should never wear your success on your sleeve. And if you do, then people probably will not want to be around you, and rightfully so. The kind of success I'm talking about creating for your life doesn't need to be worn on your sleeve, because its momentum speaks at a pitch anyone can interpret. This is the type of success that will radically change your life.

Does Having a Million Dollars Make You A Millionaire?

By definition, the answer to the above question is, yes. Logically speaking, the answer is, no. Acquiring a million dollars doesn't necessarily mean you possess an understanding of how to remain a millionaire. Amongst many studies that dissect the financial lifespan of the money a lottery winner wins, it's a consensus that most lottery winners are broke within five years of winning. Of the consistent contributing factors, a lack of financial education is the leading cause of such sudden financial ruin.

Just because you acquire certain things from your willingness to take risks in life, doesn't mean you'll stay at that high plateau. One of the starkest educations I received after attaining a true allure based on my success, is how people around you change. I feel obligated to share these personal examples, because I pride myself on not selling fantasies as a motivational speaker. I have to expose all the realities that come along with an "alluring" lifestyle.

I had a friend in particular who I grew up with from adolescence. This was my "boy," and I was always a good friend to him. Our lives were always a bit different, with me being a star athlete while we were growing up and him being more of an academic and people person. I always kept it cool with him and others I grew up with, never feeling the need to create any separation as we became older and my accomplishments mounted.

In my twenties, I gambled on myself. After playing four years of division I basketball, I decided that I would write books and become a motivational speaker. People thought I was crazy to undertake such a mature profession in my early twenties.

If destiny beckons you, running from it will only frustrate you, because your spirit knows the true you.

I went for it without hesitation. I had some very remarkable events take place in my early career. One of the most notable was having the motivational speaker Les Brown write a testimonial for my book, *The Universe Is Inviting You In*, which was released five days before my twenty-fourth birthday. It was a very fulfilling accomplishment, because the path to experiencing such a remarkable achievement was filled with obstacles, and far from a straight line.

As my twenties progressed I released more books, gained a larger following, and experienced all of the amenities of professional speaking - such as being featured on television shows and in newspapers like *The Washington Post*. The friend I mentioned witnessed all of this, seeing my struggles and meteoric rise.

For a couple of years I felt a separation happening, simply because I was a risk taker. That's what he desired, but wasn't able to find it within himself to commit to that life. Finally the inevitable happened: he no longer wanted to be around me. I saw it coming, and as he blatantly ostracized me from his circle, I accepted the writing on the wall. I wanted to ask him, "Why?" This question resulted from how far we went back. After reviewing the weeks leading up to this, I remembered him saying: "Matthew, you're flashy. You're 6'5", drive a Benz, and when you tell women you write books I know they go crazy."

Whenever I would hear statements like that from him, I would just brush them off and reassure him that he could create the same life for himself by having the audacity to try something new.

My better sense prevailed, and I obliged and pivoted from the friendship without a word. The friendship ran its course. The interesting element is, that within a few weeks, many of my friends did the same exact thing. The last friend I couldn't believe actually would do this, but simply because he saw everyone turning their backs on me at the same time, he chose to join them.

When the Writing is on the Wall, It's Usually Written in Permanent Ink!

Truthfully speaking, stardom may or may not be in my future. The writing was on the wall with many of these friends described above, but my naiveté chose to turn a deaf ear and blind eye to the truth that had been staring me in the face for years.

The truth of the matter is, that I didn't wear my accomplishments on my sleeve, but an immense amount of progress in life and the societal separation will offend people very close to you. I saw these events coming, but I just didn't want to believe them. What happened was that I was getting too flashy, to the point it began making people around me insecure. I'm here to tell you, uncommon success will do the same to you. When the writing is on the wall, pay attention to it. Imagine if I would have arrived at a place of fame, and only then figured out the true colors of those closest to me? It would have been far more detrimental, as the more success you experience, the more viscous people around you become. My only regret was that I didn't pay attention to the signs sooner, because the road to the inevitable, in this case, was littered with cautionary warnings.

The bottom line is, that when your life choices bring you increase, you can't approach your life like it is normal. I wanted to still be a member of the "crew," but my time had clearly expired. The most pivotal element in sustaining your success is understanding that, whether you like it or not, your status will change. And yes, the ladies will love you, but be aware of all of the realities that surround a meteoric rise. Always stare at the truths that stare at you, so you will have an clear understanding of everything around you.

Many people opt not to push the boundaries of life, and ravage the limits of their potential, because they still want to be a member of the "crew."

A dream pursuit comes at the expense of being unapologetic. Understand the reality that people will naturally be offended by you, even when you remain humble about your accomplishments.

If you are not afraid to stare these realities in the face when they stare at you, you are poised for greatness. If you choose to look away from these realities, your past will become your reality, as you secure a VIP seat in the sea of normalcy.

Count situations like these as "all joy." After everyone performed a perfectly- sequenced about face, one of the biggest breakthroughs in my young career took place. If you choose a higher density in life, note that not everyone will be willing to handle the change in oxygen. The path to making the impossible your norm is not easy. Your meteoric rise will attest to all, that is was worth it. What will you create?

NOTES AND INSIGHTS

NOTES AND INSIGHTS

CHAPTER 3:
APPEARANCE

Your appearance is often most the critical factor for a woman deciding whether or not she'd like to further the conversation with you. If you approach her, and your appearance is off, then you can easily make her decision for her, all without saying a word.

In the training I received to become a motivational speaker, one of the trainers told us that "we're never off as speakers." He then began to elaborate that point by saying you cannot be a believable speaker if your appearance is not always in tact.

With the herds of men who approach beautiful women, you have to set yourself apart immediately to capture her attention. Your appearance is the number one tool in marketing yourself to women. You must always be smooth. Let's begin with your clothes.

Your clothes should always have a tailored look to them. Your jeans should be fitted. I'm not talking about walking around looking foolish in skinny jeans, but rather a nice tapered straight-leg jean. Slim-fit everything is in style. Make sure your shirts are fitted. It brings out the contour of your chest, shoulders, and torso. If you remember anything from this chapter, never entertain the baggy look; it pails in allure when comparing it to a fitted look.

Your suits should definitely have a tailored look. I recommend fitted Italian suits. Even if you don't get them tailor-made for you, you can always take your suits to a tailor and have them take in the torso to give it a tailored look.

> *It's the subtleties that create the greatest impact in the minds of women. A nice fitted suit, with a fitted shirt, with Italian loafers, is the way to go my friend.*

I love wearing loafers. Your footwear is monumental, as women can tell a lot about you by your shoe game. I prefer Italian loafers to compliment anything I wear, be it jeans or a suit. Prada loafers are expensive, but they are quality and have an elegant look and feel. Quality loafers like those last for years, if you place wooden shoe trees in them after each wear. Gucci also makes very sophisticated quality loafers. Beautiful, successful, women always make comments about my Prada loafers when I wear them - along the lines of them being very impressed. The average guy in the street will not think to always put his best foot forward, in both a literal and figurative sense; by default these subtleties will make you stand out amongst the crowd.

Nice loafers and luxury cars compliment one another. If I look at a Mercedes or BMW, they very seldom change their body styles. The same is true for nice Italian loafers. Their styles are ageless. You don't have to break the bank to get a nice pair of loafers. Just wait till they go on sale at a major high-end department store, or you can literally steal a pair at a small, high-end boutique. When a small, high-end boutique has to get rid of old inventory, they sell their previous styles at extremely reduced prices, since they do not have the luxury of an outlet like a major retailer.

Subtle, but nice, jewelry doesn't hurt in attracting beautiful women either. This look is one that speaks of your momentum and allows you to appear as if you are about something in life. There's nothing like a man in a tailored suit and nice jewelry. Having women stop and stare will be your reality, if you stick to my provided script.

Get Fit

A chiseled physique is the perfect complement to fitted clothes. If your suit is fitted, you can see definition in the arms of a fit man. If your jeans are fitted, and you wear them with a nice fitted shirt, your torso will appear to have a v-shape. This is the sign of a fit man, and entices women to just hand their number over to you without hesitation.

These are the rules of the game. I did not create them, but I surely observed them. These are nothing more than my findings. Hit the gym, lift weights, play a sport; do whatever it takes to create a high value of marketability towards women. You would think this type of thing was common sense, but many men do not realize how far appearance goes towards women choosing to interact with you.

Get a trainer if you have to. Invest in yourself. Watch your diet. Beautiful women have such a variety of men to choose from, that you must set yourself apart from the crowd in as many ways as you possibly can. If you lift weights intelligently, three times a week, and get a consistent cardiovascular workout in addition to your weights, your physique can transform quickly. As your physique changes, your stock rises. Period!

Wear clothes that bring out the v-shape of your shoulders and torso. During the winter I love a nice fitted V-neck sweater from Banana Republic or Calvin Klein. If you are in shape while wearing this, it's normal for women to walk up to you, put their hands on your chest, and say, "All this for me?" I've had this happen on numerous occasions. The right physique, coupled with the right clothing, takes your allure through the roof, with beautiful women being yours to lose.

Your Face

Try not to allow your barber absences exceed a week. Keep a set of professional clippers to keep yourself trimmed up throughout the interim. I recommend Andis outliners, as they have kept many men's faces clean throughout the years. If your clothes are fitted, but your face is a wreck, it takes away from your overall allure. You want to appear as a quintessential package to women even before you open your mouth. Whatever format you like your hair and face to be, keep it styled.

Even if you do not have an acne problem, I recommend using Proactive Solution. It clears up blemishes and gives your skin a bright and even tone. Women pay attention to these subtle things that most men take for granted, or ignore. In any game, it's the in-between-the-lines things that take athletes the furthest. Attention to detail will always create an advantage in your pursuit of the things you want in life.

As far as your nails are concerned, keep them clean and neat. Women notice your shoes, and as you're sitting across from her on a date, she will notice your hands. Your hands speak volumes about you in the minds of women. It's very reassuring for them to see your appearance, head to toe, with little to no blemishes.

Oral Health

Begin by brushing your teeth and flossing very frequently. Yellow, unkempt, teeth will turn any woman off. Use a tooth paste that has a whitener in it, to keep your teeth at their brightest. These are just more subtleties to enable you to take your appearance to the next level.

I've covered your appearance from head to toe. If you implement these appearance strategies, you will almost immediately see a difference in the way women interact with you. The society we live in is very "up-front" based. Your appearance is where you make your hardest sell to beautiful women. Beautiful women naturally feel privileged due to the constant adoration by men. If your appearance is right, it levels the playing field, places her on her heels, and she will desire to know what's behind such a well-kept appearance. She's looking to be playing on her heels, as this is an unusual scenario for her at the onset of any interaction with a man. Be the man who has her intrigued before you open your mouth; be the man whose appearance destroys her pedestal, allowing her to land safely in your arms. Approach her; she's waiting.......

.....And everything else you want from life

In this visually-saturated society, people will not respect the person you declare yourself to be, if your appearance doesn't match it. I'm writing this book for men to establish a vision for themselves, and do everything within their power to achieve it.

A passage from the best-selling book of all time states, "Man looks on the outward appearance, but God looks at the heart."

Your appearance wouldn't matter, if you didn't have to deal with people in order to get to where you want to be in life - arriving at your life's vision.

Whether it is right or wrong is irrelevant, because you have to play the game of life to win your respective championship.

Whatever your vision is, your appearance must suggest that you are living in this vision, regardless of whether or not you have arrived there yet.

When I made the decision to become a motivational speaker, I benefited greatly by observing the attire of the top speakers in the industry. When I would meet them, it was apparent that they took no days off in relation to their appearance. They were always meticulously manicured and had an appearance that suggested they were living life at optimal levels of success. This is my challenge to you as well: create an appearance that suggests success is a cornerstone in your life.

You can not be a man living at his full potential unless you have a vision for your life that surpasses your current condition.

Energy Orbits of Success

Being in atmospheres of people, who are where you want to be, are energy orbits of success. I mentioned that you can take on the appearance of the type of person you want to become, simply by being around them. But you are afforded way more advantages in life than merely observing their appearance. The average person will not tell you how they got to be who they are in life, as that makes you a threat to the elite status of their success. If everyone is doing it, then there is no allure. Some people relish allure; I suggest you create it, in order to get the things you want in life, and let that be that.

When you are in atmospheres of people who are where you want to be, the clues to how they got there naturally begin to reveal themselves, if you stick around long enough. For example, I've seen Les Brown speak more than any other speaker I admire. The more I was around him, the more I began to notice subtle things about his presentation that give him his elite status as a speaker. I noticed subtle ways he sold his products from the stage without anyone being aware of what he was doing. I then implemented what I learned, into my presentations, and I suddenly began to experience similar results.

When you get into your energy orbit of success, do not go as the average person, looking to walk away with only a few tips. Go having your eyes and mind fixed to see what's not seen and hear what's not heard, and you will have what most people don't have.

The blueprints to your success are in your energy orbit of success. When you can tap into the energy that is naturally in the air when being around people who aren't dreaming, but rather living in it, you can experience real magic as the understanding of how these people are who they are reveals itself to you. When you get the understanding of something, you can recreate it.

Stay in your energy orbit of success until you reach a full understanding of how to get to where you want to be in life. You will first notice the appearance, which should be immediately adopted. When you take on the appearance of something you aspire to be, even if you have not attained it yet, you will begin to take on the spirit of that thing. When you take on the spirit of that thing, you will begin to see yourself as that person you aspire to be. When you see yourself as being something, you will confidently put energy into creating the vision you have for your life. Whatever you put energy into is what you create. The energy orbit is pivotal to you achieving your vision, because it allows you to see your dreams as being possible. When your dreams are possible in your mind and spirit, you place a creative energy into them. If you place enough energy into the things you want from life, it's only a matter of time before you live in the reality of them.

Explore the possibilities of your vision by being around those already living it. The energy orbit I speak of is a lifeline to your success. As human beings, we only place energy into the things we believe are possible. Do all you can to paint a picture of possibility in your mind. The world is waiting on you to paint your vision on life's canvas. You defeated three hundred ninety nine million, nine hundred and ninety nine thousand, and nine hundred and ninety nine sperm just to arrive here on earth. You have the power to make the impossible your norm. Believe.

NOTES AND INSIGHTS

CHAPTER 4:
LATE MODEL LUXURY

Don't believe them when they say they aren't materialistic. Many women will say that nice possessions, such as a luxury car, do not influence their willingness to interact with you. And yeah, maybe I would have believed them when I was still driving my 1994 Nissan Maxima after college. But the 7 series BMW I purchased days before my twenty-fourth birthday disproved that lie forever.

Beautiful women love luxury vehicles and all of the allure that comes with them. I can remember dating one beautiful woman in particular, who played all kinds of games while I was driving around in my Maxima. I just showed up one day in a big body BMW, and her entire demeanor changed.

Regular cars and luxury cars equate to a night and day difference in experiences with beautiful women.

If your appearance is intact and you hop out of a late-model luxury automobile with your designer apparel and sunglasses, you will see the body language of beautiful women say, "Come over here and talk to me." Whenever I go for a night out in my S-Class Mercedes it's commonplace for beautiful women to stop and wait for me to park my car, so they can start a conversation. It usually begins by them asking, "Who are you?"

I can remember walking to an after-hours establishment in DC, and engaging in a friendly conversation with two women. I asked one of them for their number, and was given the "I have a boyfriend" line. I then pulled my Mercedes up at the end of the night to pick my boy up, and the same girl who turned me down walked up to me and said "Take my number." Late model luxury will change a woman's demeanor in an instant. Is this right? I really don't think it is. But the rules of the game are the rules of the game. You picked up this book because you wanted to learn how to get beautiful women, and this, by far, is the most potent of all the strategies I've mentioned. Beautiful women love to ride in luxury vehicles, period.

Paint Pictures with No Brush or Canvas

There are unconventional ways to paint pictures with no brush or canvas. What I'm saying, is that you can get a luxury automobile for less money than you would pay for a late-model regular car. Mercedes-Benz and BMW change their body styles about every six or seven years. You can purchase a luxury car that is six years old, and it will still have all of the allure of being the latest body style and model. Whereas you can purchase, let's say, the current year Nissan, and pay the same price as you would for a luxury car that is still the latest body style. You do the math. Does she want to be seen in that 2012 Nissan, or the 2007 Mercedes? Get it? It's the allure of the game.

There are many ways to acquire late-model luxury automobiles for next to nothing. Go on websites like cars.com or autotrader.com and perform a search for the luxury vehicle you desire. Be careful, because many dealers place their cars on these sites at inflated prices. Narrow your search by clicking on "private sellers." These are normal people who are selling their automobiles at a far lesser rate than the many dealers on these sites. A private seller is usually in some sort of situation where they need to get rid of the car. Some of them are flippers, who buy cheap, and sell the car inexpensively to turn a quick profit.

I purchased/stole my S-Class from a guy who had a wedding to pay for. The price was far from what you would think I should pay for a late-model Mercedes, but he needed cash, and I had it. End of story.

You're not purchasing a vehicle. You're purchasing a level.

If you really want to purchase/steal a similar car, I suggest finding a dealer who will take you to a dealer-only auction. This is where the best deals are made. Many used-car lots make their living from dealer-only auctions. Find a cool dealer who will take you to the auction and choose the luxury automobile you desire. You will pay half of what you would at a dealer. He may charge you a fee of $500 or $1,000 to take you to the auction, but it is well worth it when you see how inexpensive the cars are.

Your allure is then complete at this point, with your presentation being at its peak, attire intact, designer shades, and late model luxury. This was my transition from night to day with beautiful women, and the same will be true for you.

When you get your vehicle, always keep it clean inside and out, as this further speaks to your level. There's no point in driving around in top-of-the-line luxury if it doesn't have a high sparkle to it. When going out for a night on the town, observe the women looking in your car, attempting to talk to you in traffic. Notice the smiles and waves you receive while in your vehicle. Absorb the reality of women waiting for you to park your late-model luxury automobile like they are your personal valet. It's pure comedy how beautiful women react to material things, but hey, I didn't create the rules; I just observe them, and report my findings.

You may not have a high-end luxury automobile at the moment, and that's fine. But begin to create the habits of someone who does. Keep your vehicle at the highest level you can, by keeping it waxed and washed, with the interior vacuumed and spotless. This speaks to your level, and is impressive to women you encounter.

Beautiful women respond to levels. The higher the level they perceive you to be on, the less barriers there are when interacting with them.

They believe they are deserving of the best, so be the best and create a match in their minds. Beautiful women will still play a game or two, but when your level is perceived to be high, in a societal sense, she'll only go so far, because she knows there are many women just as impressed with you as she is. Nice things are just an equalizer.

In totality, these are just material things, and they should not define you. There is nothing more unsettling to women than a loser bragging about his car, occupation and other possessions. Your appearance will make her want to find out everything else there is behind it. She'll see your car on the date. You're very intriguing and appealing when you can be peeled back in layers. Overall, she should be sold in you, not your material possessions, so let her discover these things in a natural way. If you lead in with your possessions, you are poised to reel in a woman who wants to use you, and take you for a hell of a ride. The kind of woman you can create something lasting with, is the one who is repulsed when a guy approaches her with a "Look at me, and all of my material possessions" attitude. She'll see your possessions gradually, so just let your up-front game impress her to the extent that she wants to see and know more. Most importantly, let her be sold on you. Materials possessions come and go, but your core-self will always be with you, my friend.

.....And everything else you want from life

When I speak of late-model luxury, I'm speaking of aiming for the highest level possible in life. My desire is that you not only create a vision for your life, but you create it at the highest level possible. When you create, go all the way with it.

There's no point in creating a vision that doesn't push the boundaries of what you believe is possible for your life.

This is the type of vision that will wake you up in the morning with a mission and purpose. These types of visions will create an unparalleled focus and determination within you. You're not living if you're not aiming as high as possible, and constantly pushing the limits of life. Choose to wake up every morning, feeling alive.

People not only deal with you on your appearance, but all of the complimentary aspects that create your level. I recently did a book signing, and my host walked me to the parking lot, and said "Which one of these vehicles is yours?" in a tone that translated to, "We see your level, but have you gone all the way with it?" This is a common question I'm asked when I speak in different places, but this is the world we live in. In my mind, I'm thinking, "Why does society determine how far they want to interact with me based on these material things that are located outside of me?" I'm not one to stare away from the truth that stares at me, so if it's late-model luxury that creates a seal of validation in the minds of people interacting with me business-wise, then it's late-model luxury I'll give them.

The Power of Levels

Whenever you have a desire or aspiration in life, your greatest ally in achieving it is being conscious of levels. Reality will serve you when you honestly assess what level you are on, to chart a realistic path to get to the level you want to get to. This is another reference to the energy orbit of success.

My only aspiration in life in high school was to play Division I basketball. I had the height, skill and athleticism to make this dream a reality. Division I basketball represents the highest level that exists in college. In my senior year, I went on visits to Division I schools in order to play with the players on the team, to see if I belonged on that level or not.

My first visit was to Liberty University, which was a low-level Division I school that had a dismal record the year I visited. I played pick-up basketball with the players, and found out that their record was not indicative of the reality of what a Division I basketball player truly is. Even before we began playing, I noticed how big these players were. Their point guard stood six-feet, four-inches tall. In the high school league I played in, most players at those heights were post players. The forwards weren't six-feet five- inches, like I was in high-school, they were six-feet eight-inches tall and above, while having chiseled, muscular, physiques.

The contrast in the size of the players from high school to the Division I level was drastic. We began playing, and I held my own against these established Division I players. Putting myself in the energy orbit of what I aspired to be, served me by painting a clear picture that I belonged there. It still wasn't that cut and dry. The end result of that reality check was my mother driving me home at 4 a.m. in the morning from the campus, and me pleading with her to drop me off at Run-n-Shoot, which was a 24-hour gym located minutes away from where we lived. I wanted to go, because even though I held my own, I saw that I had a tremendous amount of work to do, in order to play at the Division I level.

I played against players from one of the worst teams in Division I basketball, and saw how talented and athletic they were, so I knew that the better teams must have had unbelievable talent and athleticism. Getting a self-imposed reality check serves you in many ways. Most notably, it allows you to paint a realistic start line en route to your ultimate level and destination, positioning you to reach your finish line.

If you believe you belong on a level, place yourself there. Your findings will indicate whether you are ready, or whether you have to go back into the lab and improve on aspects of yourself.

Whatever your findings are, that kind of atmosphere will prove to be invaluable, as it serves as a realistic look in the mirror.

The Power of Focus

The Miami Heat won their first championship since 2006, this past season. Lebron James, the 2012 NBA MVP, is the reason why they won. The previous season they made it to the championship, only to be swept by the Dallas Mavericks, who consequently won the championship in 2011.

Lebron James faced a myriad of criticisms for his unwillingness to take shots in the fourth quarter, when his team needed him most. The Miami Heat assembled a team of superstars last season, constructed to win a championship. Lebron James was the cornerstone of this team, with the weight squarely on his shoulders to win a championship - validating him as the game's most elite player. When he fell short because of his unwillingness to shoot the ball in the latter portion of the game, when it counted the most, he faced ridicule from every possible angle.

This season, Lebron James came back to silence all of his critics with his unparalleled fourth quarter performances throughout the NBA championships. He sported a mouth piece with the roman numerals XVI, to signify the sixteen games it would take in order for him to win a championship.

When he took the court, many of the sports commentators said he had a "game face" he had never quite worn before. This was purely a reflection of his new-found focus that took greatest shape when the game counted the most - in the fourth quarter. No longer was Lebron James passing the ball to teammates who didn't share his acclaim as a player. He stepped up to the plate, single-handedly willing them to victory throughout the playoffs, until he achieved the ultimate NBA prize - a championship.

Levels are on full display in this example. Lebron James appeared in the NBA finals twice, prior to him reaching the ultimate stage of glory this past season. His focus is what allowed him to reach the NBA's highest level, and deservedly sport the crown of the NBA's greatest player.

Focus is what will allow you to excel from level to level. Focus is your ally when attempting to live the visions you see so clearly within yourself. The higher you aspire to go, the more focus is required.

Being in atmospheres of people who are where you aspire to be in life, will automatically create a heightened level of focus within you.

Uncommon focus is a trait of the uncommon achiever.

Your Time is NOW

The only thing that holds us back from achieving our vision in life is the unwillingness to focus. When you focus on the desired outcomes you want from life, the way to creating your path will reveal itself to you.

Magical events will happen around you, when you consciously create a focus on what you know you should have in life.

You don't have to wait for some magical moment to begin, before going after what you want from life, not when you possess the power to begin creating these things NOW. What sense does it make to wait for life to magically hand things to you, when you've been designed to create your inner visions?

Les Brown says, "You don't have to be great to get started, but you must get started in order to be great." No shortcoming or excuse can erase the power in any given moment, that you possess to start creating your life, your way. One of my previous books, *All We Have is NOW,* discusses the ability to create in much further detail. Life will not do things for you that you've been empowered to do for yourself. Create the focus to get started in life, and choose to narrow your focus even more, as you approach the doorstep of a place called "Destiny."

NOTES AND INSIGHTS

CHAPTER 5:
THE SUCCESS UNDERSHIRT

I enjoy having conversations with women who aren't from the metropolitan Washington, DC area. My favorite question is, "What is your impression of men in DC?" Their answers are as synchronized as cheating students. They choose their words carefully because they know I'm a native, but in so many words they suggest that DC men are very status-conscious. They lead in with what they do, their top-secret security clearance, and their myriad of possessions, as if women should just throw rose petals at their feet like Eddie Murphy in the movie *Coming to America*.

I can't do anything but agree, as I have observed this behavior on many occasions. I highlighted DC because of the elitist, well-to-do, nature of this town. This is a real "What do you do?" place, in which accomplishments are worn on people's sleeves as if they were ornaments.

My desire is for you to become a smooth man with intrigue and allure. One way to accomplish this is through creating an up-front presentation, as described earlier in the book, and at the same time being a self-assured man who doesn't allow his success to define him.

A man with vision must always stay centered within himself, in order to continually create and manifest the things he sees from within.

If you are centered in material possessions, wearing them on your sleeve, you will lose track of the core-self that will always be with you.

Success is repulsive to women when it's worn on your sleeve, unless she's looking to take advantage of you in some way. When success is worn as an undershirt, then no matter what your accolades and accumulations are in life, they will not define you. As I have stated repeatedly, when a woman can peel you back in layers, it is very appealing. If you have a vision that you are either living in, or working towards accomplishing, that alone is an impressive feat to women; so many men are content with just existing and surviving.

Imagine if you have a conversation with a woman, with your perfectly manicured and tailored appearance, and she's sold on you before your profession or accolades enter the conversation. That's smooth. Beautiful women always gravitate towards smooth, easy- going men. Believe me. She will like you more if she peels you back in layers. If the inevitable question of occupation comes up early in your initial conversation with a woman, don't go into a networking spill, divulging every detail about what you do. Talk in a quick, straight, line. If she wants to know more, she will ask.

Insecure Vs. Secure

The insecure man leads in with the enormity of greatness that surrounds him. His occupation, salary, and possessions will immediately come up in conversation. Most often this information will not be solicited by the woman. This kind of guy is insecure, and women know it. The secure man will let the wonderful embodiment of who he is come out gradually and naturally. Your decoration of accomplishments should be the icing on the cake. If you are secure within yourself, your confidence in who you are, and not what you possess, will create all the required intrigue in a beautiful woman's mind. This will immediately compel her to want to further the conversation with you.

The Real Conversation

The real conversation is the one that doesn't physically take place. If your appearance is constructed as I described previously, then her mind is already spinning as to who you are and what you do. **You don't have to wear your success on your sleeve when your appearance has a strong allure.** The appearance I described is meant to set you apart, and make you a star in your own right. Not stardom in the regard of the bright lights of Hollywood, but more so in a way that separates you from the appearance of the average man.

If your allure is right, she knows you're wearing your success undershirt, even if you don't go out of your way to let her know you're wearing it.

The power in interaction will always be in what is not said. The beautiful woman wants the man who can create intrigue without saying a word.

If you can do this, you place her in the not-so-familiar position of being on her heels. Her beauty usually allows her to view men as desperate suitors, as she looks on from her pedestal.

Every beautiful woman desires the man whose embodiment makes him the object of her affection. There are just so many talking bobble heads in her face all day, that she desires you - the breath of fresh air, the man with the vision who possesses actual substance, and the man who can intrigue her. If you adopt the principles in this book, she desires you, my friend.

.....And everything else you want from life

Although painting pictures of success is important in life, my desire is that you become the best man that you can possibly be. Self-Actualization, which sits atop Maslow's Hierarchy of Human Needs, is a repetitive theme throughout this work. Its repetition is present because self-actualization, a deep-seeded belief in yourself and your infinite possibilities, is the cornerstone of a solid man.

Dr. Wayne Dyer says, "When you choose to trust in yourself, you are choosing to trust in the same wisdom that created you." My interpretation of this is that we all come from an all-knowing, omniscient Creator, God. We all have an extension of our Creator within us, and when we choose to trust in ourselves by not allowing things located outside to define us, we connect the pure power of God within - allowing us to be the best man possible.

It's difficult to trust in yourself, and be content with who you are from an internal awareness, if you are constantly seeking things outside of yourself for validation. If you are content with yourself, and not afraid to follow the visions that you see from within concerning the unlimited heights you can take your life, you have a natural wisdom internally to guide you to the various destinations of life.

A perpetual chase for accomplishments will blind you from the clarity of vision that will allow you to create your life, your way. There's no reason to embellish or wear your accomplishments on your sleeve, to impress anyone, when you are centered in yourself. People brag and boast when the wrong things hold weight inside of them. There's something to be said about an individual who has "made it," by all accounts of the material world, and hasn't allowed that to change their demeanor at all. When success doesn't make you feel high-minded, it can easily be accredited to a strong sense of self. Successful, cool, people are a pleasure to be around. Who really wants to be around the person who lies, inflates, and brags all day?

Constantly having to let people know what you do, and who you are, is feeling the need to compete. A person with a strong sense of self doesn't feel the need to compete.

If you are who you are, and the next man is who he is, where does the need to compete come into the equation?

I had to learn this as my success became more apparent throughout the years - when I started feeling competitive vibes from people I least expected. As the allure of your success becomes more apparent to people, and they begin to compete with you, you have the choice to just remove yourself from the equation. Insecure people will often attempt to engage you in conflict when your success outshines theirs, in their eyes. Remember. There is no conflict without two willing participants. Keep a still demeanor no matter how much success you attain. Real success speaks at a volume that anyone can interpret, all without you having to say a word.

Your True Identity

To identify with anything located outside of you, is to set yourself up for disappointment. The only constant life deals us, is change. If you choose to wear anything on your sleeve, you identify with it. Life is full of ebbs and flows, and ups and downs. What benefit does identifying with anything in the material world create for you?

Always stay true to yourself and the vivid imagery that your inner spirit reveals to you, concerning who you are. If someone attempts to discredit what you believe is possible for your life, politely pivot from them. You must always maintain a strong sense of self, for you to arrive at your vision.

I make these statements, because every major success I've experienced has come as a result of going in the opposite direction of the opinions of people who did not share my vision in life. In high-school, people said I wouldn't get a Division I basketball scholarship. I did. In college, my professors openly labeled me the black sheep of the English Department, saying they didn't think I would graduate. I excelled in my upper-level course work and graduated with a book contract. When in my early-twenties, people said that my books wouldn't sell. Two are endorsed by legendary motivational speaker Les Brown, and have sold all over the globe.

Those examples are not meant to shine light on my accomplishments, but rather to expose the possibilities of your life - when you choose to stay true to yourself and your sense of vision, with no outside interferences. The only obligation that we have in life is to be who we uniquely are. Believe.

The Power of Self-Development

Self-development is consciously engaging your mind towards absorbing messages of possibility, to create what you want from life. Self-development creates an uncommon story in your mind, to empower you to create the uncommon dreams in yourself.

The law of the world is to survive and be content with just enough.

The uncommon man fights to create an uncommon story in his mind, so he can rise above the norms of society.

When I faced negative opinions early in my career, my greatest ally was taking in messages from my favorite motivational speakers daily. The positive messages I absorbed created a barrier against all negativity and opinions that did not line up with me achieving my vision in life.

Self-development is life's checks and balances system, as negative messages pertaining to your dreams, get checked out at the gate of your mind.

Self-development keeps you humble as well. Pride constantly wants to flash success; humility doesn't flash, because there is always another plateau to be reached.

Self-development encourages you to avoid plateaus in life, always creating a mental atmosphere to imagine an even larger vision for your life.

This can be equated to a professional team which expects nothing more than to win a championship. Championship teams have a very short memory for both wins and losses. They don't get too down on themselves when they come up short, and they don't get too full of themselves when they experience victory. They celebrate only when they win their championship.

There is always a championship to be experienced in life, since we are created with an ever-evolving nature. A higher level of achievement is always possible, as long as we have breath in our lungs. Never sell yourself short by celebrating too early and plateauing. Keep your undershirt intact, and sleeves spotless.

NOTES AND INSIGHTS

CHAPTER 6: ENERGY

When you approach and interact with a beautiful woman, you have to learn to read her energy. If she is interested, you will notice by how she engages you in equal conversation. Women have no problem being close to you as well, when they are interested, and they may touch you in flirty ways.

To the contrary, if she is not interested, you will be able to see this in her demeanor. Her body language is standoffish, and her facial expression is displaying annoyance and non-interest. Some beautiful women believe the world revolves around them, so as soon as you feel an unfavorable energy, just walk away. Even mid-sentence if you have to. Abruptly end your sentence and say, "It was a pleasure conversing with you." If her energy is just egregious, simply walk away without saying a word.

A woman's energy is always on display. Your strength in getting beautiful women is to read it quickly.

Everyone deserves a match.

Obviously, you are interested in her if you approach her. She knows this; either she will match your energy, if she is interested, or she will not provide the complement in energy that creates a match.

If a woman's energy suggests she is undecided as to whether she wants to interact with you, don't ask her to further the conversation. You approached her without any question marks in your mind, so for her to display indifference toward you is showing that there's a miss-match in energy.

Confidence

There is no exact formula for getting beautiful women, since no two people on the planet are exactly alike. You will have to continue to approach beautiful women until you find out what works for you. The more women you approach, the more your confidence will grow, as your understanding of what makes them tick becomes imbedded in your mind.

This, in turn, will create a confidence, which translates into a swagger. When you are comfortable, and no hesitancy is present, when approaching beautiful women, it creates intrigue in a woman's mind. It's called being smooth.

When you are smooth, you can immediately turn a "maybe" into a "yes." If your allure is intact, you can talk in very straight lines to her and be believable. Sometimes beautiful women are interested in you, but they feel the need to challenge you, based on most men's adoration of them. This is the part of the conversation where I tell women, "Let's be real, you know you want to give me your number." It usually works if your up-front game is intact. I say things like, "There's no point in us lying to ourselves ...you're sexy ...I'm sexy ...so why don't we just do the inevitable?"

Most men are afraid to say these kinds of things to beautiful women. Any man who has the audacity to speak to her this way, has an intrigue she has probably yet to experience. This kind of dialogue immediately destroys the pedestal men have built for her, and places you two eye-to-eye, with her in a position to make an immediate decision.

It doesn't hurt to be cocky when dealing with beautiful women. In reality, a confident man is the only one who can hold her attention anyway, because of the adoration she receives every minute of every day by those who will give it to her.

You must display finesse in your approach and interactions with beautiful women. The right action, for the right situation, allows you to master getting beautiful women. If you two share a strong energy, there's no need to be cocky, because she has intentions of furthering the conversation. Those types of interactions call for you to be smooth.

If you sense a little hesitancy, and she's displaying a slight indifference, but you can feel it in your core that she's leaning towards giving you her phone number, just express to her straight-lined truths like, "We both know you'd like to further the conversation just as much as I'd like to."

Talking to beautiful women in straight lines will often tip the scale in your favor.

When you encounter the beautiful woman who says she'll take your number, just pull out your business card, hand it to her, and let that be that. You must always have a business card on hand. Don't ever get caught without one, as you never know who you will encounter on any given day. This action places the continuation of the interaction squarely on her, with no games involved. If she likes you, she'll call you.

Be Strategic

If your life is structured in a way that you are working towards a vision, you have to read energy quickly. Everything you do in life, even your interaction with women, has to be calculated. When dealing with beautiful women, you have to read energy from the beginning, or she will engage you in a chase that takes precious energy away from where it serves you best - your vision.

I did not write this book to create pimps and players, but rather men operating at optimal levels in their life, in terms of getting the women they desire – along with all of the finer things life has to offer.

You will learn to read energy by default, if you can learn to see what's not seen, and hear what's not heard, in your interaction with women.

The body language that leads to a "yes," "no," or "maybe," will become apparent almost immediately after your initial interaction.

If you are a man with a vision, you don't have time to waste. Reading energy is your greatest ally in protecting the creative space that's necessary for you to create your life's vision. The best-selling book of all time says, "Where there is no vision, the people perish." The corollary to this is one of my favorite original quotes: "Where there is vision the people flourish."

The Chase

I can remember running into a girl I had dated two years prior. She seemed excited to see me, and hit me with the "Nice to see you again," text message shortly after our encounter. But all I could do was think back to the "cat and mouse" interaction we had when we previously dated.

Initially, we sat down over drinks and just conversed, as we got to know one another. I called her afterwards, got no response, and the interest consequently faded. A few days later I got the "What's up stranger?" text message. I texted her back again, only to get no response in return. So the interest faded again, only to get the "What's up stranger?" text message a couple of days later. That was pretty much it after that.

This woman was just how I like them: Tall and beautiful. Considering my height, she knew we were the perfect match. Our initial hug, when we went out the first time, felt right. We were, aesthetically, a match. Beautiful women love to play games. This is how they categorize guys, even if they like them.

This was her way of seeing if I would chase her. Most guys will chase a beautiful woman, resulting from a lack of belief in themselves. If you have to chase them, there is no match. When you see there is no match, disappear.

If a woman plays games in the beginning, she'll play them all throughout the relationship.

Some men like this sort of thing, but if you are a man on a mission in life, these types of interactions are cancerous to your future.

So, here are this woman and I seeing each other two years later. I figured I didn't have anything to lose by giving her a call. I called her the day after we ran into one another, to say "What's up?" and catch up a little. I heard back from her two days later and she said, "I saw you called." We briefly caught up, and set up a date for that Friday.

Initially I was hesitant to set up the date, because in my core I felt we had no energy. I remembered our interaction two years prior being a game of cat and mouse. Couple that with the fact it took her two days to call me back, and the writing was on the wall.

The day we were to go out rolled around, and that morning I called her. I let her know that I believed we just didn't have any energy. I was cool about it, as I let her know that neither one of us were bad people, we just didn't have a spark. I then reminded her of the game of cat and mouse that took place years prior. She claimed she really couldn't remember. In the end, she said she respected my honesty, but still thought we should go out. I just didn't feel it, and suggested that I would let my instincts prevail.

When the writing is on the wall, pay attention to it, as your instincts will become increasingly sharper, the more women you interact with. You want the kind of beautiful woman who lights up when you call or text her. That's momentum my friend, with the makings for a smooth interaction. You will know when a woman really likes you. Deal with these women.

If you adopt the right appearance, and began making progress to creating something worthwhile in your life, you can easily let go of the women with whom you share no energy.

I'm offering suggestions for you to become a marketable product. If you become this type of man, the pick of the litter will desire you.

I could let this breathtaking beauty go, because I have experienced the allure of the game. Beautiful women approaching me, has become a staple in my life.

When you walk down the street, and a woman can instinctively feel something alluring and different about you, she'll let you know she'd like to interact with you.

When this is your reality, you'll have no problem only dealing with women you perceive to be a match.

The guys who chase beautiful women are not respected by them.

When a woman attempts to engage me in a chase, and I suddenly vanish, she knows exactly why, without me saying a word. This way, if she comes back in the picture, she knows not to play the games she plays with the other men - who are there on bended knee, at her beckoning call. She ultimately wants a solid man she can feel secure with. If you chase her, you appear weak.

Staying in the Flow

When you have energy with a woman, she will keep you in the flow of the things you are creating for your life. The average man would still interact with a game-playing-woman if she is beautiful enough, because people who don't have high aspirations are usually just playing in life. If you are content with being average, you can chase as many women as you'd like, giving away precious energy that could be devoted to creating something for your life you have yet to experience.

"The flow" is effortless. She *will* call/text you back in a decent amount of time after you reach out to her. She rarely cancels on you. There may be a hiccup or two in your dealings with one another, but overall you have a good flow. This is energy.

The Spin Move

I can remember dating a woman who was a game changer. She was the personification of the woman I described in chapter one. Men would literally say slick stuff to her in passing, when I was beside her, as they just couldn't help themselves. Men with their wife and kids would stop and stare. She was a certified banger.

We hit it off quickly, experiencing a very fun week of dating. At the end of the week she began to fade. She asked me to dinner and we sat down. We conversed, and I said I noticed things had changed a little. She made up some excuse about her career taking her possibly out of town, and she didn't want to get attached to any man. This was an attempt to make an exit. I responded with, "Oh, that's cool. We'll just be the kind of friends that say hello if we see each other out and about."

When a beautiful woman attempts to make a spin move, let her. The average man, with a woman this gorgeous, would make a fool of himself trying to convince her to stick around. When the energy fades, you no longer have a match. Everyone deserves a match.

Right on cue, she emails me a week later saying, she doesn't like avoid speaking to people who are her friends, and she hopes we're cool. I emailed her back saying, "We're cool for sure." The energy had faded, so there was no point in rekindling the interaction. Sometimes you will have a fun week, month, or year with a beautiful woman, and that's cool. When the energy fades, just disappear; there's another beautiful woman just waiting for your approach.

It never ceases to amaze me how, even when a beautiful woman desires you, she'll still play games. In the above example, when the woman said the stuff about not wanting to get attached, she was making her exit. What need was there for her to reach out to me a week later? I was still on her mind, and maybe she wanted to pick the interaction back up. Go where the energy is.

360

Life comes full circle. I was out on a date with a very tall and beautiful woman, who many say upon first glance, was a perfect aesthetic match for me. I hadn't said one word to the girl in the above example in a year. Almost a year to the day I saw her in the establishment I was at on my date. I walked in, appearing alone, as my date had already arrived and was in the restroom. I said hello to her just as I said I would do if I ever saw her anywhere else. Right after that, my date walks out of the restroom, with a beauty that putting on makeup would detract from - she being so natural.

Moments later my date and I were out on the street, and happened to run into the girl I had dated a year prior. The way the setup was on the street, we were all in very close quarters. The girl I dated a year prior couldn't even look at me and the beautiful girl I was with this evening. She completely turned her back to us.

There's always another beautiful woman, when you find that a match is not present. Always know, in your core, that you deserve nothing less than a match.

Don't be a game player, and don't tolerate games.

Be a solid man, and create an atmosphere for the beautiful woman to appear, with whom you share energy.

.....And everything else you want from life

World-renowned pastor and author Mike Murdock says, "Go where you are celebrated and not where you are tolerated."

With an abundance of gifts, talents and abilities embodying every human being, what sense does it make to subject them to people who don't celebrate them?

The key to creating a successful life is to always be on the lookout for a match for your gifts and talents.

People who tolerate you, are people who don't see your dreams and visions as clearly as you do. People who celebrate you, are people who welcome your gifts with open arms, and celebrate the things you have to deliver to the world.

I can illustrate this belief by observing the life of Jesus. Please allow me to preface this saying I am not attempting to influence your religious beliefs, or make religious arguments through this observation. I am far from religious, but I believe there is a tremendous amount of wisdom to be absorbed when dissecting what was behind the legacy of Jesus.

In the Bible, Jesus performed some of the greatest miracles known to date. When Jesus was on the earth, He was uninhibited spiritual energy, meaning that He was a walking miracle. Everywhere His feet tread, He had the ability, the capacity, and most importantly the desire, to perform a miracle.

Many times throughout the Bible, Jesus was poised to perform a miracle, but couldn't due to passages such as, "He departed, because they received Him not." When He wasn't received, He simply departed. He didn't try to convince the people that He was a walking miracle; He simply pivoted and continued moving forward until He found His match. Essentially, what inhibited Jesus from performing miracles, was when people did not match His energy.

The miracles He was able to perform were the result of people's belief in who Jesus was, and what He brought to the table. When He found His match, miraculous feats were the norm.

I submit to you today, that you have a miracle inside of you in terms of the limitless possibilities that encompass your gifts and talents. When you find your match in the form of people who believe in you, you will then find your miracle. There is a capacity within you to perform feats that would blow your mind, and that of everyone around you.

The force of destiny is waiting for you to believe in yourself and your limitless creative power, so you can be introduced to your true unlimited self.

Your miracle is in your match.

The Truth about Life

This past Christmas eve, my family did something we had never done before. We had a Christmas Eve gathering at my sister's house. At this gathering were my mother, father, siblings, aunts and extended family from my sister's side of the family, as we do not have the same mother.

Going into this night, I knew that my most memorable experiences would come from my Aunt Brenda, her never-ending love for me, and the belief I was the most handsome man in the world. All I can remember from this night is my Aunt Brenda taking pictures of me, and complimenting my articles she read online, from different publications I write for.

Fast forward to one week later, and my mother informs me that she has something to tell me. This is never good, so I listened intently. She said, "Your Aunt Brenda passed away." I couldn't believe it considering I had just seen her days prior.

What is the truth about life? The truth about life is that it is short and fragile. It makes no sense to place yourself in situations where the gifts and talents you were sent here to deliver to this world are not on full display.

It makes no sense to suppress the miracles that are inside of you - when the world needs to feel your impact.

I have confidence in saying that Jesus was the greatest man to ever walk the earth, for reasons totally separate from religious belief. I judge the greatness of a man by the legacy that he leaves. No other legacy exists today, that is greater than that of Jesus Christ. No other legacy has permeated the ages, like that of Jesus Christ. This, in my mind, qualifies Jesus as the greatest man to have ever walked the earth.

The Way You Move

When Jesus knew it was His time to change the course of history, He moved with precision, and wasted no time. When He wasn't received, He performed a spin move so quick, Hakeem Olojuwan would have to bow down. Jesus was always on the hunt for His match. I submit to you today, that your greatness hinges on your ability to never settle for anything less than a match in what you desire from life. Place your miracles on full display, where they belong.

Reading Energy

If you can read energy, you can master the game of life. You will know people who celebrate you by the way you are received. If you see side eye's complimented by bad vibes when you are around a particular group of people, this lets you know that is an environment where you are not wanted, and simply tolerated.

If people have a welcoming energy, and are receiving of what you embody, you have found a match. You aren't just dealing with people in life; you are dealing with the energy they possess. Similar energy between individuals sets the stage for real magic to take place.

In terms of your success, your maximum effectiveness is achieved by staying in the flow. The flow is achieved by being in environments where you are celebrated, and by quickly removing yourself from environments that pose resistance to you. This is living life with precision and creating the highest likelihood of experiencing favorable outcomes.

Reading energy quickly not only serves you in getting beautiful women, it shows you how to navigate life effectively.

Precision is moving with an intelligent quickness.

Life is nothing more than a game of situations. Reading energy quickly will always land you in favorable circumstances. You will always be at your best when you find a match in energy.

Confidence

Be who you say you are, and be confident while doing so. When you are in the necessary environments you must be in to get ahead in life, always display confidence. Being sure of yourself doesn't just impress women, but people as a whole. Confidence emits an energy that makes people feel secure in dealing with you.

If you are in an environment where your confidence is perceived as a threat, you are bigger than this environment, and have to find your match elsewhere.

There's no room to grow in circumstances like these. There's a difference between being brash and arrogant, and being confident. If you are brash or arrogant, expect people to avoid being around you. If you display confidence, and people are offended, chances are they envy the trait in you, and have not found the confidence to pursue what they want from life.

People who aren't intimidated by confidence, are secure people. Secure people usually stay in the flow, because they don't feel the need to pose a resistance to people who show the ability to accomplish special things in life. I'm writing this book so you make the impossible your norm.

By surrounding yourself with secure people, who aren't threatened by your ambition, you are setting the stage for greatness.

Finding environments where you are free to be yourself, with no outside interferences, will catapult you to greatness. Your greatness needs no restraints in order to reach its full potential. If you have to portray yourself in a lesser light than what you really are, you are shrinking. You are either moving forward or backward at all times in your life. Stagnation is an illusion.

You can live a life of greatness by always being aware of the energy around you. Assess the energy quickly, to see if it serves you or inhibits your growth. If the energy is right, explore the possibilities of what you can create. If you do not have a match, pivot towards the environment which compliments your greatness. Never be afraid to be yourself.

The only obligation we have in life is to be who we uniquely are. Be you, with no apologies.

NOTES AND INSIGHTS

NOTES AND INSIGHTS

CHAPTER 7:
THE DATING GAME

I would first recommend dating only women with whom you share energy, as described in the previous chapter. Leading into a first date with a beautiful woman having momentum, ensures you won't have an extreme amount of guess work to do attempting to figure out if she's feeling you.

Don't just meet a girl and go out with her. This could potentially be a waste of time. Have a conversation with her to make sure you two are on the same page in terms of what you are looking for at the moment. You don't want her thinking you're someone she can have a long-term relationship with, when all you have to offer at the moment is something casual, or vice versa. I've wasted plenty of time, energy and money dating women to get to know them.

Precision living is getting to know her and her desires before you two are on a date.

A conversation is nothing more than feeling her out to see if she's someone you'd like to further the conversation with, in terms of dating. If you two do make it out on a date, don't do anything extravagant the first time. Even if it's no secret that you're loaded financially, do something low-key the first go round.

You never want to set lofty expectations in a beautiful woman's mind. Some, but not all of them, are used to having the whole world shown to them early on in their interaction with men. Even if they are not into a guy, some will still take them for a ride to see what they can get out of him, for as long as they can. This is how to avoid being that guy.

Doing something unassuming and inexpensive on a first date allows you to see if she's into you. If she is into you, she won't mind. If her expectations were a wined and dined experience, like she's accustomed to, and you feel a resentful energy towards you for not doing so, vanish. You don't want to get caught up with a user. Many beautiful women live their life allowing their beauty to get them whatever they desire, with men bending over backwards to accommodate them.

A regular first date subconsciously lets the woman know that you are meeting her eye-to-eye. This is an approach you want to take with beautiful women. They are used to having their beauty being viewed in a light of superiority by droves of men. Subtly level the playing field with an eye-level approach.

After the date, do not succumb to nonsense like the two day rule before you call her. If you are feeling her, reach out and say you had an enjoyable time, offering the invitation to do it again. If you two share the same sentiment, you have real energy and should see where it goes. If you don't feel the same energy coming back your way, after letting her know you'd like to enjoy her company again, and then fade.

Never try to create something that isn't there, when you have the power to create the favorable outcome you desire, simply by taking a different shot.

Your Space

The urging to create clear expectations in the beginning of an interaction with a woman is critical to your overall success in life. Early on in the career of my favorite basketball player, Kobe Bryant, he was a stone cold beast. His skill set allowed him to make a mockery of anyone who attempted to guard him. Later in his career he was dubbed "The Black Mamba," which is the deadliest snake on the planet. Although he still possessed the same skill set he had earlier in his career, as an athletic scorer who was coming to break you, he became aware of the places on the floor where he was the most effective as a scorer.

The vision I urge to create throughout this book will develop when you make a conscious decision to create it. You will find your way. When you find your way, you find your rhythm in life. When you convey to a beautiful woman what your expectations are, they should be centered on keeping you in rhythm.

There's nothing worse than being honest and straight forward about what you are looking for in with a woman, and she acts like she's ok with it - only to try and get you to compromise towards what she is looking for. This is a game of control in dating; a game I urge you to vacate as soon as you realize it is taking place. You cannot create your vision in life if you do not possess a creative space.

When your space is compromised, a detour from your vision is inevitable. The severity of a detour is seldom understood at its onset.

You may be able to find your way back quickly, or the severity of getting off track may lead you to a place where your initial destination becomes a distant memory.

The Tennis Match

Tennis is one of the only major sports that can be played professionally, as a single competitor or with a teammate. Dating is the same way. Some people choose to only date one person at a time, while others opt to test the waters. Individually, you should do whatever option makes you comfortable. Personally, I have found some of my greatest revelations about women, and what I ultimately desire, came by dating more than one at a time.

Ideally, if you had the woman you desired, you wouldn't be out there dating. A major objective for a single dating person is to find their match.

There's nothing wrong with placing more than one rod in the waters, to strengthen the probability of catching your ideal fish.

If you are dating more than one woman it's not something that has to be broadcast to every woman you date. The reality is that neither one of you belongs to the other, and are both in the process of finding a match. If she asks you if you are dating anyone else, be truthful. You don't want to complicate things when you are dating. Ideally, you shouldn't want to know this until you are ready to propose a desire for exclusivity to her. It's almost implied, if two people are dating and single, there are likely other people in the equation. Do what works for you.

Real Magic

Sometimes the rules just don't apply. There are women out there who will captivate you after a first date. A deep understanding in your core will dismiss any notion that this was an ordinary encounter. The initial spark you two shared upon first encountering one another will quickly culminate into an explosion. This, my friend, is real magic. If it is a shared emotion, it can be intimidating for both of you, but go with it.

In a case like this, do not be afraid to let a woman know that you are willing to put everything else around you into exile, and see where you two can go. I say this because connections like these are rare. I've had about two in my lifetime; they are well worth exploring the possibilities of where they can land you. Place all egos on the backburner and let the girl with whom you've experienced magic, know.

Life doesn't deal us many moments like this, so go all in. When you know that no other woman around you compares to the one you desire in your core, go for it.

We only have one shot at this thing called life, so express gratitude for moments of perfection when life deals them to you.

When you meet this type of woman, you can go to a place where you are surrounded by other beautiful women, and it's as if they don't even exist. She's your every other thought, and her grip on your heart is tightening with every passing second. This is the one where the exploration of the world of women around you must come to a halt. When the thought that she could be "the one" enters your mind, and when this is a seldom- entertained notion with the normal woman you encounter, go for it!

.....And everything else you want from life

Kanye West is one of the most self-sufficient musicians on earth. He has the catchiest lyrics, which are listened to with an air of expectation for each word. He also possesses the ability to create the most vicious of beats, for which musicians pay him millions of dollars. At some point this musical genius' rope ends, as others have to enter the equation, to make him the world-renowned musician he is.

A one-man-show can only go so far in life. My desire is for you to create a large vision of success, and bring in the right people to help you arrive at your vision. In order to do this, you will have to go on a few "dates," so to speak. When you are building something in life, you always want the best people to help you construct it. When I was just starting as a speaker, one of my mentors gave me a great piece of advice. He said, "Work with people who spend eighty-percent of their time in their core genius." He was saying to work with people who are who they say they are.

A mistake I made early in my career was taking people at their word, in terms of the services I needed to create my vision. Do your homework before you get in bed with people. Don't fall victim to "This is a family friend" or "This person came highly recommended." Make sure people have a proven expertise in their craft, and solicit more than one person to ensure your final decision brings you the best bang for your buck.

Choose to Evolve

The way I dated beautiful women in my early twenties is drastically different from the way I date them in my late twenties. This is due to the accumulation of knowledge I have gained throughout the years, and my willingness to take something away from every situation I find myself in.

When you take away insight from the various experiences of life, you accumulate knowledge, which in turn creates personal evolution.

Your mindset should never stay the same from year to year. By taking something away from dating experiences, it gave me a clear picture of the women I ultimately would like to interact with. It also determined the type of dating I was willing to undertake with a woman.

Personal evolution is a choice, as you have to choose to go through life fully conscious to learn the unspoken messages at your disposal on a daily basis. Avoid repeatedly finding yourself in the same undesirable experiences, by allowing each life lesson to make you sharper in your understanding and movement throughout life.

Personal evolution was never meant to have a ceiling. It is a potential life-long process. No matter how many accomplishments you accumulate, and how much knowledge you incur, understand that you will never completely arrive until your last breath is taken. To have feelings of arrival is to consciously create opposition to your true nature - which is to evolve.

Space

Having a vision, and making a conscious decision to create the necessary environment for it to happen, are completely different things.

The most magical moments in life occur when you chart a path to the road less traveled.

Mistakes are inevitable when you begin this journey, but after a while you while you find the rhythm and cadence which suits you best, giving you the most honest shot at creating success.

Your creative space is your greatest ally in creating your life, your way, and fulfilling your vision. When you get serious in life, distractions will present themselves to you almost on cue. That friend from out of town will pop up on you, and a myriad of other things will suddenly attempt to make their way into your space.

If you compromise your space, you compromise your race.

I'm not saying you have to disappear into exile somewhere. However, I am suggesting that when you are in a critical creative state, abide accordingly. It's difficult to birth anything without the proper environment and conditions.

The longer you stay on the road less traveled, the easier it becomes to understand which environment encourages you to stay on it.

When it's time to buckle down and create your vision in life, understand that most people opt to not live their life this way. This is not an "us" versus "them" mentality. Rather, it is one to create an understanding that many people are just out here playing. When it's time to be serious about your vision, you cannot choose to play and think you will still arrive at your destination.

The $100,000 Man vs. The $1,000,000 Man

The average man would see a yearly salary of $100,000 as a sign of arrival. This financial accumulation can make a man feel like he's accomplished something in life. Notice I said "the average man." This book is written for you to err on the side of the uncommon, and dismiss all aspirations of being average in life.

A couple of good friends I hang with from time-to-time are the six-figure type, with salaries of $100,000 plus. I gravitate towards these friends because they are secure within themselves, and I never sense an energy of competition which I have grown accustomed to when hanging around males my age.

They diligently go to work, and put in their time. I have nothing but respect for these friends. They have amassed an education and display skills on the job which warrant such a salary. But after getting off of work these friends simply play. That is the extent of their life - which is an ideal life by society's standards. But what if they put energy into creating something even greater for their lives, which could land them one more "0" in their yearly earnings?

In my observation, you can be in the right career field, and catch a few breaks to find yourself in the $100,000 category. It is not as easy to trip and fall into the million dollar category. The difference between a six-figure earner and a seven-figure earner is the distribution of energy.

If you can consciously choose to focus your energy into creating your vision, and not parking when you reach society's standard of security, six-figures, you can realistically attain a seven-figure income.

The traits of a seven-figure man are vision, discipline, non-complacence, and intelligent distribution of their energy.

You can trip and fall into a six-figure salary, but the same does not hold true for the seven-figure yearly financial accumulation.

8... 8 ... 8

While on TV with legendary motivational speaker, Willie Jolley, there was a simple question posed to him, for which he gave a profound answer. The question was, "What advice do you have for the public in the economic climate we are currently facing?" Willie Jolley replied with, "You have eight hours to work, eight hours to pursue your dreams, and eight hours to sleep."

Although survival is real in an economy like this, there still lies the ability to make progress towards the bigger picture for your life - if you are willing to develop one.

If you don't have the time to pursue your dreams, then you don't see enough value in their pursuit. We all make time for the things we value in life.

The brilliance in the 8 ... 8 ...8 answer, is that it creates a clear picture of how to distribute your energy, if you opt for an extraordinary dream-filled existence. You don't have to get off of work and play, although some play is essentials to your overall sanity. We are not robots. The free eight hours of a day serve as a blank canvas, with you possessing the power to paint your vision onto it. What will you create?

NOTES AND INSIGHTS

CHAPTER 8:
PLAY TO WIN

I can remember meeting a very beautiful woman, with whom I shared an intense immediate spark. I love interactions like these, because they have a built-in momentum without the nauseating middle stage of elongated dating. She was my ideal woman. When we met, the attraction was undeniable. To my surprise, our first phone conversation lasted an excess of four hours. We had a real, but rare, immediate connection.

After this phase, we began filling each other in and learning about the personalities that comprise us as individuals. The shared sentiment between us was, "Where have you been my entire life?"

One day, as we were on the phone, I asked her to hold on for a second, as I had to take a quick business call. After I had been on the other call for a brief period of time, I could hear her hang up. After I wrapped up the short business call, I called the girl back and asked her if she seriously hung up the phone after me clicking over for mere moments. It was no secret that I was in business for myself full-time, and that in order to make a living, I received calls at all hours.

I talked to her very honestly and in a non-confrontational manner. I told her that I had kept it cool throughout our magical interaction, and had given her no reason to pull that move. I then went on to say how smooth our interaction had been, and that little stuff like that had no place in something as natural as we shared.

She replied to me that all the guys she's encountered her entire life would have called her back and apologized, after she hung up on them. She then reminded me that that's why she liked me so much; she was enamored that I was different than the doormats she'd dealt with her whole life - those that would lose their sense of self, and let actions like those go unchecked, out of a fear they may lose her.

Believe me when I say this woman was extremely beautiful. She looked as if she stepped off of someone's runway. Every guy she encountered lost their sense of self and walked on egg shells in order to not lose her pretty face.

This game of life was meant to be played to win, and was never intended to be played with a mindset of playing simply not to lose.

When you play not to lose, you lose automatically. You can't enjoy life in its fullness if you are not going "all in" at whatever you do.

You've heard me say, "Be solid," repeatedly throughout this book.

A solid man is one who is not enamored with a beautiful woman's looks, to the point he just lets her do anything, is the one she will fall for.

It is so rare, that it will put her on her heels, in an unfamiliar position from her normal pedestal.

With beautiful women having the world handed to them for as far back as they can remember, it's not a matter of *if* she will test you, it's *when* she will. When she tests you, never change your composure. Always talk to her in straight lines, conveying the truth, and she will thank you for it. Who wants a doormat as a potential mate?

I have a million stories like this one. Hearing so many beautiful women tell me the same thing, when they attempt ill-advised moves, convinces me that most men compromise themselves for beautiful women.

I've seen men who I thought were solid, get involved with beautiful women and totally lose their sense of self. I've seen men tolerate some of the craziest behaviors in the world to keep a beautiful woman around. Surprisingly, these were men I never thought were capable of bending in such a manner.

You have to trust your instincts when dealing with women. If you turn a blind eye to actions in an interaction, she knows in her mind that this is something she can get away with. These behaviors, left unchecked, open the door to more irrational actions. Before you know it, you will be a doormat, just happy to show off such a beautiful woman to the world.

When you lose your sense of self, the world around you becomes distorted. Clarity of yourself and the world around you begins with a strong sense of yourself, being centered at your core, and not allowing anything to break it.

You have to be clear about what you can and cannot allow into your atmosphere, in order to be a high-achieving man in life.

Your terms of engagement should be adhered to, and never compromised. A girl who believes she's entitled, with the world at her disposal due to her looks, can quickly and easily throw your world out of whack. When she knows she has her grips in you, get ready for a tremendous ride.

As aforementioned, detours from your path in life are very dangerous. Finding your way back from a detour in life is not a given. You always want a woman with a good spirit and internal balance. You want your woman to be self-assured, as this decreases the likelihood she will throw you off balance in life.

To be fair, if you desire these attributes in a woman, you should possess them yourself, or else you run the risk of throwing her off balance. A solid man understands it takes more than a pretty face, and will not join himself to a woman who doesn't complement the goals he has for his life. I am writing to the man who has a vision and wants to continue creating a larger vision, and also to the man who wants to establish a vision for his life.

These types of men cannot compromise when it comes to the type of woman they interact with, no matter how beautiful she is. A model of perfection is one of the greatest illusions that exist in life. You two will both make your mistakes due to being human beings. There's no need to slam the gavel on a woman if she exhibits an undesirable trait. If she's not willing to change then the red flags should begin to appear.

In my experience, when litanies of red flags continuously appear, it is just the makeup of the woman, and it gives you clearance to disappear. If your world is centered on getting beautiful women, then you are probably open to continuing an interaction after a woman displays less-than-favorable behaviors. If you are centered in your vision, then your non-negotiables are your non-negotiables.

There's no time to waste if you are on your way to a destination in life. When you know in your core that things probably won't work out between you and a woman, exit gracefully.

Always close doors gently, as life has shown me that gently closed doors often lead to wide open opportunities.

Some beautiful women cannot wrap their minds around the fact that a man would *voluntarily* just end an interaction with them. They will try to keep coming back because their ego must prevail - meaning you must not go anywhere. They will act as if they are on board and can flow with the energy of your life, only wishing to tip the scale back in their favor. This only forces you to deal with the same behaviors that prompted you to exit. After you have seen the same thing over and over again, just be a man, and accept that this is who the girl is, and move on.

The woman will eventually get the message, and you will thank yourself when you encounter the beautiful woman that complements you, and doesn't throw your world off balance. Always be a clear headed, smooth, man. This allows for clarity to be your constant companion. When clarity of mind is a fixture in your world, the things you can create for life are endless.

A congested consciousness suffocates the dreams and desires you possess for your life.

Clarity creates an atmosphere of peace; peace creates creativity; creativity manifests the highest desires you have for your life. Will you be the man who is awe-struck and satisfied with a pretty face, or will you be the man who wants a complementary inner-beauty of depth and substance? The answer to this question has a strong bearing on the altitudes you will reach in life.

The Highest Fulfillment

The highest fulfillment, is living life and keeping the flow of interactions between you and other people, on terms that keep you in the flow. When you play not to lose a beautiful woman, and bend the rules that would ensure you optimal levels of fulfillment, and you actually are setting the stage for failure. A successful interaction is one that doesn't disrupt your atmosphere. When you choose to engage in, and continue, an interaction that creates an imbalance, you are robbing yourself of the opportunity to find an interaction with a beautiful woman that keeps you in the flow.

This is a classic case of playing not to lose. When you play not to lose, you deny yourself the opportunity to find what you are looking for, on your terms, thus winning. You deserve to win in life. The only way to win is to not settle for something you deem undesirable.

> *The reason why you see the man with the flawless woman, but miserable in the relationship, is due to that man's lack of belief in himself. He believes that he will never find a woman as "bad" as her again in life, so he denies himself an optimal connection in favor of nice, shiny, trophy.*

My desire is for you to be a self-actualized man, never compromising his desires for the allure of a pretty face. A self-actualized man is clear on what he wants from life, and knows how to maintain an atmosphere to encourage the flow of highest desires. If you had a pretty face, you can get another. It wasn't a fluke that you landed the woman you desired, in terms of looks. The pretty faces you land in life are a byproduct of something you possess at your core.

You can lose a beautiful woman, but you can never lose the essence of yourself that drew her to you.

I'm not saying it's easy for every man to let a beautiful woman go, even when he knows their time has passed, but it's definitely necessary. You never want dead weight attached to you as you ascend to your life's destination. If you had her once, you can get her again, this time with a more desirable makeup.

Do what brings you fulfillment, when it comes to interacting with beautiful women, and hold true to this. Always be sold on yourself, and the world of beautiful women around you will fall into its natural place. The highest level of fulfillment in life is experienced when we don't bend on our desires. If this posture is maintained, at all costs, your highest desires will be your tangible reality. Believe.

.....And everything else you want from life

In my senior year of college, my basketball team played the University of Hawaii. This was probably the most memorable game of my senior season as a collegiate basketball player. At halftime we lead the University of Hawaii by twenty-six points; a lead that seemed insurmountable, by all stretches of imagination. There was nothing but laughs in the locker room, as we knew we had the game in tow. Our coach instructed us to essentially hold the ball, doing the exact opposite of what had garnered us the immense lead.

I'm guessing the University of Hawaii's coach instructed them to turn up the defensive intensity, seeing how we were totally embarrassing them on their home floor. Being down twenty-six points, they had nothing to lose; they trapped us and applied some of the most intense defensive pressure we'd encountered the entire season up to that point.

Their strategy worked. We attempted to pass the ball around passively, and did not attack the basket like we had done to create the lead. The huge arena filled with their fans roared, as they forced us into turnover after turnover. All the while we attempted to hold the ball and protect our increasingly-fading lead.

The momentum completely shifted in our opponents' favor that night. It culminated into a loss, at the hands of us losing the largest halftime lead I ever could remember us building. The emotion in our locker room was one of utter disappointment and shock.

Throughout the remainder of the season we experienced more downs than ups, ending with an all-too-familiar losing record at the end. We lost in the first round of our conference tournament. On the bright side, spring break was days away.

I was home in Maryland for spring break, relaxing with a beautiful young lady, when I received a call from the athletic director from the university I attended. They informed me that they were strongly considering not bringing my coach back next season as the head basketball coach. Even though I no longer was an athlete for the university – not since my last game - they showed class by informing me of their decision to consider firing the coach.

When I returned to school after spring break, our entire team was summoned to a conference room in the athletic department building. The athletic director informed my teammates and I, face-to-face, that the university decided to part ways with the coach. The decision came with an explanation, as the coach had one year remaining on his contract. Essentially, they wanted him out of his position so badly, they paid him the remainder of the money that was left on his contract for the next season, and hired another coach to take his place.

The reason the athletic director gave for his firing was that there were too many instances when we had the lead late in games, and played not to lose, instead of playing to win. The concern was that my coach's mindset was to abandon the very things that allowed us to gain the lead. While playing it safe, to his admonishment, he blew lead after lead, and compiled loss after loss.

What sense does it make to hold the ball for dear life, and attempt to play it safe? Anything worthwhile in life will always require risk. If something is worth working for, don't hold back. Continue to do it, and look for ways to do it at an even higher level. If you accomplish something and "hold the ball," you are limiting yourself - Create an even greater outcome of success that could supersede anything you have yet experienced.

When you don't play to win, you automatically play to lose. If you think you are holding the ball, you are actually moving backwards.

You are either moving forward or backward at all times in life. Stagnation is an illusion.

Be Clear on What You Want

Fulfillment in life, is having a clear picture of what you desire, and imposing a barrier to anything that tries to enter your world and is not in concert with this image.

Life is miserable when you know you are settling for less than what you really desire. It's miserable because something in your core knows that you have the power to make an honest attempt at the things you desire from life.

Compromising, out of a fear of taking a risk, is the behavior of the majority. The average person will stay in a situation they dislike, as long as they can maintain familiarity with it, and security from it.

The Dream or the Job?

As a motivational speaker, I hear countless people telling me how much they hate their jobs, and how much they would love to live their dreams. I love the Willie Jolley 8... 8....8 example of the illustrated distribution of time throughout every person's day. Jobs are essential in this economy, but you will never begin charting a path that leads to your dreams, until you see value in living your dreams, and display a willingness to begin moving in their direction.

We always put our energy into what we value. When the dream has more value than the job, you naturally will begin immersing yourself into creating your dreams. What was once leisure time after a hard day's work will become your dream-building time, as you begin to do what it takes to transition form the job to the dream.

If you see value in something long enough, you will give a disciplined amount of steady energy to it - giving yourself a fighting chance to create it.

Are there areas of your life that you accept, knowing they are not what you really desire? The answer to this question will determine the likelihood of change occurring in your life. Average people settle; great people create. The world-famous motivational speaker Les Brown says, "You can make a living, or live your making." Living your making is choosing to pursue the desires from within, until you live in them. Desires haunt you because you were designed to live in them.

Comeback Power

Life will deal all of us unfortunate events which, from time to time, temporarily set us back. Losses are as inevitable as the changing of the seasons.

In order to lose something, you must have previously possessed it. If you possessed it once, you can create it again.

Always choose to come back from adverse circumstances. It is within the scope of who you are, to do so. Adverse circumstances need your permission to be labeled as final.

There are an unlimited amount of comebacks in you, if you don't succumb to unfavorable events and circumstances.

Live from the reality that your essence is what attracted anything you will ever lose in life. You may have lost a tangible thing, but the essence and understanding of how to recreate it is your most valuable tool in exercising your power to come back from anything.

Live the fulfilled life, on your terms.

NOTES AND INSIGHTS

NOTES AND INSIGHTS

CHAPTER 9:
PLAY YOUR HAND

Every man does not possess the looks of a Ralph Lauren model, the height of an NBA shooting-guard, or the chiseled physique of an Olympic sprinter. However, one thing every man does possess is the physical hand that God dealt them.

Women are experts at highlighting their best aesthetic features, and crafting an appearance to accentuate the best cards they were dealt.

In attracting beautiful women, it's advantageous to tailor an appearance to highlight your best physical qualities.

In my opinion, every man has something going for them physically, that can attract the woman he wants.

To begin identifying the best cards in your hand, you must first embrace the hand you were dealt. It's common for me to hear a grown man say that he would rule the world if he had my height. It's a compliment that I appreciate. My overwhelming sentiment towards these remarks are that these are grown men with no chance of ever growing further, but they still have the very live cards that God has dealt them - these can be played in their favor.

When you accept your aesthetic hand, it then becomes alive to you. When it becomes alive, you begin to see the possibilities of how to play your cards in the best manner to create your desired outcomes with beautiful women. Chapter three discussed the power of appearance, but grasping the power of the physical hand leads to a higher mastery of yourself, as you connect to the hand you were dealt, and understand the limitless possibilities you have in playing it.

The Concrete Truth

The concrete truth is that whether you are short, tall, or fall somewhere in between, your stock rises with beautiful women when you are in shape. Not too long ago, I was out at a very popular night spot in DC. I saw a guy who was decent looking and not the most vertically gifted. What this guy did have, was what any straight man would call a "banger" on his arm. She was a 5'9" beauty with a physique that could mentally reiterate how many wars have historically been started over women. She was flawless, and even though the club was still shaping up in terms of patrons, she was hottest thing by far that night.

What this guy did have going in his favor was that he was jacked. He had the muscle definition which alluded to very few lapses in his gym visits. He wore a tight-fitting Armani exchange t-shirt that wasn't anything fancy. But, it was clean and stylish, and most importantly, it brought attention to the best cards in his hand.

If you are an able bodied man, being in the best shape you can possibly be in, is a non-biased, attainable goal.

Whether you are short, tall, fat or skinny, the path to creating your best physique can begin at any moment.

You may not want to shell out the cash for a gym membership, so explore alternative ways of enhancing your physique, like investing in an Olympic-style weight bench from your local sporting goods store. It's free to run around the block frequently throughout the week. If you value maximizing ways to enhance your physique, you will do whatever it takes to do so. Of all the things you can do to up your physical stock with women, this is it. This physical enhancement is totally in your hands, and can be fueled by commitment and effort.

You know your hand better than anyone. If you have nice broad shoulders, highlight them. If you have pretty-boy eyes, then wear colors that enhance them in the eyes of women. If you're tall, don't fall victim to the popular adage that this is enough in the eyes of women. Take it to the next level, and don't appear slinky, as if the weight room is foreign to you. Put on a little bulk so you don't look awkward. Wear stylish clothes too. It's almost expected that tall guys don't have style.

If your face isn't the easiest on the eyes of women, make sure you are manicured to the 9's, with a meticulously-stylish appearance. Some people are dealt a hand that requires more work than other men, and that's totally cool. Just be honest with yourself and stare your hand in the face.

> *An honest in-depth look at your hand will allow you to have a realistic perspective on what it takes to play it in the best light.*

The Prolonged Look

It's ok to admire another man's hand. This is a sign of internal security, and of a good life attribute by not having a jealous spirit. Ultimately, women gravitate towards the man who is secure within himself, no matter his appearance.

If you find yourself taking an elongated look at the hand another man was dealt, you will be blind to your own live cards.

Accept that life will not deal you every physical card you desire. There's no such thing as a model of perfection. Underneath it all, everyone has something they'd like to improve about themselves. Accept the gifts you've been given physically. Enhance the ones you can change, and accept the one's you can not. This translates to fulfillment in life.

Be You

Do not be the man who lies constantly about who he is and what he does for a living. Beautiful women take men's best shots all day, every day, so just be blatantly honest about yourself. You may not have the flashiest of careers, but if you have adhered to my admonishment on creating a larger vision for yourself, it will be evident to all that you are on your way to creating a better situation for yourself.

Don't try to become something you aren't, to impress women. It's tempting too, being in the presence of a woman who can make time stop for most men. The best thing you can be is cool, calm, and collected when talking to a beautiful woman; the best thing is to be you, and stand behind whoever you are. If a woman can't accept you for you, there is no match. The truth always reveals itself eventually. In totality, you don't have to live and die with beautiful women; you have to live and die with yourself.

.....And everything else you want from life

There's no getting around it. We are all dealt a hand in life. From our physical attributes, talents, capacities, and innate way we see and navigate our way through life. This is what comprises our life's hand.

In observation of the many lock outs which have taken place throughout the last year in the ranks of professional sports, many people have said phrases like, "If I was making that kind of money, I would just shut up and play." The owners of these various professional teams want players to take less money, and the players are fighting for what they feel is due to them.

Underneath it all, these athletes are in a multi-billion dollar market, of which the pie is divided amongst very few athletes, who comprise the professional ranks. They are the elite of the elite, and their "hand" affords them access to that type of income. It's tempting to label these athletes as greedy for fighting for what is theirs, but in reality, their battle is in proportion to the hand they were dealt.

Liberation and total freedom in life occurs when we stare reality in the face, in terms of our hand, and embrace it as what we have to work with.

Steps to fulfillment are guided with an appreciation of yourself, and the many unique cards you possess.

If you were at a casino attempting to play a card you didn't possess, a look of perplexity would grace everyone's face. Playing with the cards in your hand places you in a realistic lane of possibility. Imagine how much "envy" would subside in society if people admired another person's hand, even if it contained cards that would never appear in theirs.

When you have a realistic perspective of yourself, and view your hand with an appreciative outlook, it then becomes alive to you. When it's alive, the possibilities become apparent. The perfect blinders to your life's possibilities are framed in a prolonged look into someone else's hand, while still holding your own live cards.

Personal Power

A fitting description of personal power is accepting the cards which are concrete and changing the one's which aren't. To personalize this: you can't make yourself taller, but you can take measures to make yourself leaner in appearance.

When categorizing your cards into two piles - one being fixed and the other being changeable, mastery of your personal landscape will begin to reveal itself. Overall, your stronger cards will become apparent. In most card games, playing your stronger cards and eradicating your weaker ones, proves advantageous in the scope of creating a favorable outcome.

Pertaining to the cards you currently possess, that are neither concrete in nature, nor to your liking, embrace the power to change them. The ability to create change is in the fabric of us all.

The Power of Clarity

Accepting your concrete cards, and taking measures to change the undesirable ones that can be changed, creates an internal peace. Peace, in turn, lends itself to internal clarity, as your strong attributes gain relevance in your mind. This clarity and renewed belief in yourself encourages an atmosphere of change. If it's a "genesis" you wish to experience, it begins with a realistic assessment and an empowered perspective of yourself.

If you desire a corroded, unrealistic reality, just keep your lens fixated on the abundance of other hands around you. If you truly desire to bleed your hand for everything it's worth in this lifetime, play your hand with tunnel vision; be sold on yourself, and watch the depths of your personal greatness unveil.

A recurring theme throughout this work is the Hierarchy of Human Needs, in which world-famous psychologist and philosopher Abraham Maslow stated that self-actualization supersedes all other human needs. Self-actualization can be summarized as oneness with, and awareness of, one's self.

Your personal power and door to the limitless exists in the perception you have of yourself. Your greatest fulfillment in life resides in playing your hand ad nausea daily, and simply being you.

Your Strongest Card

While I was attending a seminar by world famous motivational speaker, Tony Robbins, he spoke life-altering words that I will never forget. "This is the most competitive era in history. Being good or great doesn't cut it any more; you have to be outstanding."

Your strongest cards are your effortless gifts, which are distributed to all human beings before arrival on earth, and which serve as a blueprint to your destiny. A gift is something that is far superior to anything else you do. It comes natural and effortless. The intent for receiving these gifts was for you to live in them freely, and exhaust all the possibilities for them thriving on earth.

See God

If you can learn to see God, and understand how He communicates with us in terms of our assignments to fulfill on earth, you will understand the blueprints to your destiny. I asked myself the question, "Where do I see God in His most pure form in the earth?" My internal answer was that I see God in nature. Nature adheres to its Creator's instructions to thrive. It evolves and changes on schedule, with no barriers or interferences in consciousness. It simply is God.

Since nature is God. I asked myself, "Where do I see God in every human being?" The word "natural" is derived from the word "nature." Consequently, the God in every human being must be what you do naturally.

The key to understanding your destiny is to understand how God, the Creator of every human being, communicates with us in terms of our destiny. If you defeated 399,999,999 of your brothers and sisters to be the one who won the race, made it to conception, and was birthed... this is a clear indication that you have a purpose in life.

The effortless natural gifts are clear indications of what your purpose is in life. There's no logic as to how you are great at some things, while being average at others. Even though rhyme or reason can't explain this, the force of destiny is at the wheel of your effortless gifts.

I referenced the Tony Robbins quote because you always want to place your best foot forward in life, giving you a fighting chance of excelling and breaking the walls of society's box. If you are outstanding at anything, without question, it is going to be rooted in your effortless gifts.

The Opportunity in the Recession

Tony Robbins quote, in reference to this being the most competitive era in history, is entrenched in the reality that our current economy is in recession. There are more qualified workers for jobs than there are available opportunities. Many educated and experienced workers are underemployed, working jobs that society suggests they are overqualified for. This reality exists because people are just trying to feed their families, and are taking necessary measures to do so - even if it means menial work.

The competition arises when millions of qualified workers are fighting for the shortage of jobs they are more qualified to work. It's even more competitive when you look at the reality of what it takes to survive in a recession.

This is the hour of the person who is willing to take their life in their hands, and choose to live their dreams.

Throughout this recession, I have seen countless family members and friends lose their jobs due to no fault of their own. With less money in circulation, many companies were losing profits at such a rapid pace, that letting go of employees was the only way to stop the economic bleeding.

If you choose to identify the best card that life dealt you in terms of your effortless gifts, and create your way financially from it, you have a fighting chance in this recession. Play your best card in this economy, as this ensures you the greatest probability of creating your life, and your way through this economy.

I often asked myself, what would have happened to my friends and family members when they were fired, if they would have had something else they were working on, in addition to their jobs.

In life, inopportune circumstances do not have to be setbacks, if you prepare accordingly.

With the only constant in life being change, how could you realistically place all of your eggs into one economic basket?

On so many levels, it makes sense to live your dreams in this climate. If you lose your job, but you have already built momentum working towards your dreams, then what could have been a setback is nothing more than an opportunity to pivot into what you were destined to do anyway.

You can't afford to rely on one stream of income, and not explore the opportunity of living your dreams. Don't be the man who gets off of work, and wastes the free eight hours we are all given in a day. Build something greater for your life.

One of my friends was fired because he was the newest hire, and the rest of the employees had been there longer than him. They figured he was young and had no dependents, making him the company's sacrifice, with no fault of his own.

A family member of mine served her company for a significant amount of time. Her company was bought out and placed under new management. Even with exemplary reviews from the previous management of the company about her, the new management couldn't see a fit for her in the company any longer.

Is this what you want to subject yourself to in this economy? Play the best card life has dealt you, in terms of your effortless gifts. It is not an easy road to live your dreams. However, I can promise you that it is worth it to test the limits of their possibilities.

If you have been on the fence about living your dreams in this economy, this is the hour to climb over it, into new terrain for your life. Tunnel vision will serve you on this path. This is an average world we live in. Do not expect average people to relate to you when you opt to travel the road to your personal greatness.

The opinion that you respect in terms of what is possible for your life, is the one you will create. If you respect a sidelined voice, that isn't even in the game you are choosing to play, you will be right back on the sideline. You will be joining the majority who opted to play it safe in life, suppressing their inner greatness. If you respect the voice of your Creator, whose nature in you is to do anything but fail, you will arrive at a place called, Your Best Life Possible. Believe.

NOTES AND INSIGHTS

CHAPTER 10:
EGYPT OR GENESIS

One of the most empowering things we can do in life, is come to the realization that many things will culminate - creating the opportunity for us to create various genesis on our journey. The seasons of change are inevitable, as change is the essence of life.

The reiteration of finding a match throughout this book occurs because we all deserve a woman who complements us, just as any woman deserves a man who complements her. Matches make life smooth, and provide a foundation that stands solid through the many types of ebb and flows.

"Egypt" is a term I associate with a season which has clearly passed in one's life. "Genesis" is the new beginning that we all have the power to create.

We all will encounter interactions that we know are over.

Even when we give it our best shot, some things just aren't for us, no matter how bad we want them to work.

When we come to this realization with a woman, it's always best to let her go - or take up residence in Egypt, occupying space in a season which has clearly passed.

It's ok to fight for what you believe in, when wanting to preserve a relationship with a woman. When you know in your core that you've exhausted all of your efforts, and "that thing" just isn't present in your relationship, embrace your power to create a genesis.

This situation is one that is not foreign to me, as I have found myself at the crossroads of staying in Egypt with women, or creating a genesis. Many times I would think I was ready to let go, only to connect with something deeper, which pushed me to stay in the relationship a little longer. But then the inevitable would happen; I gained a clear awareness that it was over, and that we were both on borrowed time.

Operating on borrowed time takes time away from the genesis that sits before you. The ability to create a genesis, in terms of finding the type of interaction you truly desire with a woman, is always at your disposal.

Average men settle for relationships they know don't suit them; great men are unafraid to let a woman go in order to find the match they not only desire, but deserve.

Look Forward

It's tempting to look back at women who represent Egypt, after you've chosen to create a genesis. My personal experience has shown me that when you interact with women who you left in Egypt, you will quickly find out why you left them there. The very actions and characteristics that caused an internal tipping point are the same ones that will resurface.

Trusting your instincts is vital to clear navigation in life.

If you repeatedly see something in a woman that is a deal breaker, urging you to end the interaction, do so. There's no point in rationalizing behaviors that repeatedly surface, when you know in your core that you desire a woman with a different essence. Compromising what you desire in a woman is the gateway to non-fulfillment. If you see something repeatedly, it's for a reason. Your instincts are derived from the spiritual essence we all possess. Not paying attention to them, in most cases, will land you in a position you could have avoided, if you would have just listened to the voice within.

You will encounter women who are in no way bad people, but just not right for you. The temptation to call the girl who you left behind for good reason, occurs when it seems like your options are few. I'll be the first to tell you that these moments represent a crossroads when you must choose to go back to the oppression of Egypt, or takes steps forward to creating the paradise of a genesis.

Paradise

When you leave women in Egypt, and choose to create a genesis by exploring possibilities with other women who could be a match, almost on cue, Egypt will try to make their way back in your life, to rob you of a potential paradise experience. Matches with women are paradise-like experiences.

When you make a conscious decision to leave a woman who represents Egypt, by some stroke of the unexplained, you will somehow be approached by Egypt, as you make efforts to move on.

There's no guarantee that paradise awaits you when you choose to leave women who represent Egypt behind, but at least you are positioning yourself for a potential paradise experience. When you encounter a true paradise experience, with you and a woman being the perfect match, you will understand the extent of captivity Egypt had you in, and the freedom genesis has brought to your life.

When Egypt calls, don't answer. This is a literal and figurative statement. After coming to a clear realization that a woman you've interacted with is Egypt, let all remnants of her go. I'm talking about phone numbers, text messages, and any other items that link back to her.

This is letting the remnants, and most importantly the energy, of Egypt go.

As long as you entertain any facet of Egypt, it subconsciously still has a hold on you.

Go all the way with it - understanding that a genesis is a new beginning, that is lived in its fullness when remnants of Egypt are nowhere near your person.

Always have the mindset that paradise could be right around the corner. I won't sell you a fantasy, saying that everything you believe will manifest in your life. I will present to you the truth that letting go of seasons past, opens you up to receive a genesis experience, which could become your paradise.

Egypt may try and get you to feel sorry for her, and

explore many other slithery angles to get back into your space. You will regret taking the bait when a clear genesis desires you, but is holding back because she knows that something else has a hold on you... and she's totally open for a genesis experience with you, rooted in no past baggage.

Travel Light

When you leave Egypt behind, disengage yourself from her memories. When you physically leave Egypt, it doesn't mean you have mentally left Egypt. Mentally leaving is a byproduct of choosing not to harbor resentment towards women who represent Egypt. Understand that you two didn't have a match, and let that be that. Wish them well, as this frees you up spiritually, allowing you to have no leftover baggage filled with regret or resentment.

Have love for all the women in Egypt. Disdain and ill-feelings toward the women in Egypt often surface in you towards the woman you desire a genesis with, in the form of making her pay for the sins of Egypt.

Smooth men travel light and are always open to the possibilities of what could be. I'm not saying the experiences of Egypt don't take a toll. We are human beings above all and have what all humans have - emotions. Choose to let go completely, and master the personal landscape that encourages the flow of a genesis into your space.

Be thankful for every woman in your life who represented Egypt. Your interaction could have been three days, months or years. The bottom line is that she made you more aware of what you really desire, and gave you momentum towards finding that, if you let her go.

Life will ultimately take away from you, or you will choose to take away from it. Reflect on Egypt and the circumstances that placed a woman in the land of Egypt in order to take away valuable lessons, and avoid experiencing things you deemed unfavorable.

Reflection serves you. A prolonged look backwards blinds you from the possibility of a genesis.

A trained eye that recognizes Egypt, is the only eye that can recognize a genesis.

.....And everything else you want from life

If your current situation does not suit you, create a genesis. The continuous urging to leave any situation that reveals itself as Egypt, takes place due to a genesis that is urging you to create it.

The mastery of movement is the mastery of life. Understanding when a season has passed, and moving accordingly, will place you in your correct season with pinpoint accuracy.

Destiny's Dance

It is the design for every human being to take risks.

Delving into new territory means that you are forced out of your comfort zones. It is only then that you evolve.

Evolution is the intention behind the existence of every human being.

I was recently in a television studio with a relationship expert who is a good friend of mine. He had a young lady and me in the studio that day to record video blogs that he would send out to his subscriber base, and place on his website.

I was no stranger to the television studio, as I am the co-host of a show titled: "How to Survive in a Bad Economy", which airs in my hometown of Prince George's County, Maryland, as well as in Washington, DC. The young lady who was in the studio with me was visibly nervous, and asked me to rehearse her segment with her. I gladly obliged, and I served as her lone audience member as she practiced her material in front of me.

She continued to focus on the fact that she was extremely nervous, with this being her first time doing something of this nature. It dawned on me that being nervous is a positive emotion. Nervousness means that you are entering new personal territory, and positioning yourself to evolve as you were intended to do. I explained this concept to her, and she saw her nervousness in a new perspective. After a couple of takes, she nailed her segment, becoming more comfortable with every take.

I submit to you the question, "Have you been nervous lately?" If you haven't, then maybe you haven't explored new territory in a while, and tested the boundaries of life which could unveil a genesis.

Destiny's dance is taught by an instructor named Faith. She teaches very elusive dance movements. To onlookers it appears as if you are taking steps backward, but when the dance is over, it is apparent to you and every onlooker that you have taken a gargantuan leap forward.

The logic of the world is to play it safe, and hold onto the security of the familiar for dear life.

The majority of the world lives in Egypt, even though the thought of creating a genesis is a constant companion. It's a constant companion because our nature is compelled evolve no matter how numb a person has become in the world of the average.

When you opt for change in your personal life, it is only natural that you encounter opposition. When you go against the majority you will encounter opposition. Creating a genesis with your life, and testing the boundaries of what is possible, makes a visible target for naysayers, because you are operating at a higher, but visible altitude.

I can remember making a decision to write and publish my first solo book *The Universe Is Inviting You In,* days after I graduated from college in 2005. Everywhere I turned, I encountered opposition, entrenched in a belief that I could not pull it off because of my age. I even had a religious figure that I admired and respected say to me, "What makes you think you can do this? I haven't even done it yet." This person spoke as if they were the barometer against which I should measure my ambitions in life.

Needless to say, I continued writing in silence. My silence was not the result of shame, but rather of a focus that didn't seek validation from average people, living by the average laws that govern the world.

My book was released five days before my twenty-fourth birthday, with a testimonial from world-famous motivational speaker and author Les Brown on the cover, because he liked my book enough to put his name on the line for me.

You never know what is possible for your life when you opt for a genesis over the land of Egypt. If you are not encountering opposition, you are just like everyone else - playing it safe in life. Opposition, in the pursuit of something greater in life, is validation that you are headed to a place of greatness. If you don't look, act, and smell like the majority, then get ready to be challenged.

The people who pose the most opposition, are people who choose to remain on the sideline, while they clearly see you in the game. You are in the game when you are pushing the boundaries of what is possible for your life, being willing to create the various genesis you see within yourself.

Being a young African-American man in my late twenties, who speaks to audiences across the United States, and is the author of five books, being challenged is now a way of life. Some people are blatant about it, while others take a passive approach.

I have come to see the deeper meaning behind challenges. Challenges are an indication that you are a threat to someone. People do not normally challenge people who they believe are average. I know if people aren't blatantly challenging me, then I am not exercising my power to create a genesis.

Inhabitants of Egypt will always challenge people in the land of genesis, because this, deep down, is where they want to reside - and they resent you for making it out.

Never take a challenge personally. They are nothing more than validation that you are moving in the right direction.

If you put energy into addressing a challenge, you are moon-walking back to Egypt. The land of genesis always has forward movements.

Don't just hear the voice of your challenger; see where the voice is coming from. It will be more than evident that the voice is below you, coming from the sinking quicksand of Egypt.

There is more to you than you could ever imagine. New beginnings are always at your disposal, for as long as you have breath in your body. Always choose to fly in the lane of possibility. You have the power to create any genesis you see within yourself. Believe.

NOTES AND INSIGHTS

NOTES AND INSIGHTS

ABOUT THE AUTHOR

MATTHEW C. HORNE, motivational speaker and author, is the president of Optimum Success International, a speaking and publishing company located in the metropolitan Washington, DC area. He is an international authority on Maximizing Human Potential. Matthew is the author of *The Universe Is Inviting You In*, and *All We Have Is NOW*, which are both publicly endorsed by legendary motivational speaker Les Brown. He is also the author of *Choices: The Young Black Man's Guide to Successful Living* and *How to Get Beautiful Women ....and Everything Else You Want From Life*. Growing up, Matthew's ultimate vision for his life was to play basketball in the NBA. He positioned himself to live this reality through obtaining a full-athletic scholarship to play Division I basketball in college. Much to his surprise, destiny revealed his true calling during his collegiate years, as he discovered a passion for motivational speaking. Matthew was told by his professors he would never make it as an English major, and to the astonishment of everyone, he not only obtained a Bachelor of Arts Degree in English, but was offered his first book contract before he graduated in his last semester of college. Matthew's message is one of creating your own reality according your vivid destiny pictures. Matthew empowers audiences to live their unique truth, independent of the opinions of others. Matthew's message is quickly spanning the globe through his books, audios, and motivational speeches. He is a writer for the *Washington Post's* "The Root DC" section. He is a staff writer for *EmPower Magazine*. He is the co-host of the television show "How To Survive In A Bad Economy." He has also been featured on the legendary radio station WOL with his weekly minute motivational segments. Matthew is also a regular contributor the internet's leading motivational ezine: *Let's Talk Motivation*. Matthew will bring any event to life! Matthew is available for speeches, radio and television interviews, and book signings. All who encounter Matthew C. Horne will leave with a heightened awareness of their limitless possibilities, and be positioned to live their Best Life Possible.

To learn more about Matthew C. Horne, please visit www.matthewchorne.com

SERVICES

Motivational Speaking:

Matthew C. Horne is the world's premier motivational speaker and leading authority in Maximizing Human Potential. His message has spanned the globe and will bring any audience to life through an awareness of their limitless possibilities and creative potential. Matthew is available for speeches, lectures, seminars, and radio and television interviews.

Testimonial:

Thank you very much for your recent motivational speech on "Peak Performance in the Workplace." I am very appreciative of what you delivered to our employees here at NASA Goddard Space Flight Center.

You brought your experience to the table and stressed teamwork. Your entire presentation was value-added. In a brief period of time, you stressed how employees can achieve peak performance by valuing their work and bringing their best work and attitude to everything they attempt.

—Michael P. Kelly
Chief, Institutional Support Office, NASA Goddard Space Flight Center

Professional Speaker Training:

Matthew C. Horne provides training to individuals who aspire to be cutting-edge professional speakers. Matthew shares his knowledge that has allowed his message to span the globe, with every speaker he trains. If you desire an education in how to cultivate, package, and deliver your message to the world, look no further than Matthew C. Horne. Contact Matthew at matt@matthewchorne.com to set up your free consultation.

Testimonial:

I took Matthew C. Horne's speaker training course and it helped me a great deal. I was able to launch my Motivational Speaking Business and hit the ground running based off what I learned from Matthew. His training helped me to place 3rd out of 3,000 Toastmasters in the 2011 District Speech Contest. This training is a must for anyone who aspires to speak professionally.

Eric M. Twiggs, Motivational Speaker
2011 Division E Toastmasters International Speech Contest Champion & and District Finalist
www.ericmtwiggs.com

Book Publishing Service:

Matthew C. Horne will publish your book in three weeks, plain and simple. His publishing team will take your finished unedited book document and turn it into a professionally published book in lightning speed. The level of publishing Matthew C. Horne provides his clients allows them to immediately carve out a significant space in the literary industry.

Testimonial:

"Matthew C. Horne, through his publishing service, worked with me to create a book that can grace any book shelf, with a look and feel that can rival books published by major publishing houses. Matthew C. Horne's publishing service was exactly what I needed in order to get my book published in a quick, quality manner. Matthew is the answer to your publishing needs."

-Frank Love, Author of How To Gracefully Exit A Relationship

ALSO BY MATTHEW C. HORNE

Available at www.matthewchorne.com

$17.00 USD (ISBN: 978-0-9794550-0-1)

Testimonial:

"The Universe Is Inviting You In is a great tool on the road to your destiny. Each of us must choose our path and utilize the knowledge and wisdom that is guiding our journey from within, giving us the power to live our dreams."

-Les Brown {The Motivator}

Available at www.matthewchorne.com

$17.00 USD (ISBN: 978-0-9794550-1-8)

Testimonial:

"All We Have Is NOW...is a powerful guide which inspires us to rise to the occasion of being the great, creative and unstoppable beings that we were originally designed to be...offering valuable insights on how to leverage and build on the most precious moment set before us...NOW!"

Les Brown
International Speaker, Trainer & Speech Coach
www.lesbrown.com

Available at www.matthewchorne.com
ISBN: 978-0-9794550-2-5

www.ingramcontent.com/pod-product-compliance
Lightning Source LLC
Chambersburg PA
CBHW051944160426
43198CB00013B/2294